T0358602

Russian Corporations: The Strategies of Survival and Development

Russian Corporations: The Strategies of Survival and Development has been co-published simultaneously as *Journal of East-West Business,* Volume 6, Number 4 2001.

Russian Corporations: The Strategies of Survival and Development

Andrei Kuznetsov
Editor

with the collaboration of Olav J. Sørensen

Russian Corporations: The Strategies of Survival and Development has been co-published simultaneously as *Journal of East-West Business,* Volume 6, Number 4 2001.

Routledge
Taylor & Francis Group

LONDON AND NEW YORK

First published 2002 by The Haworth Press, Inc

2 Park Square, Milton Park, Abingdon, Oxfordshire OX14 4RN
605 Third Avenue, New York, NY 10017

Routledge is an imprint of the Taylor & Francis Group, an informa business

First issued in hardback 2020

Cover design by Thomas J. Mayshock Jr.

Library of Congress Cataloging-in-Publication Data
Russian corporations : the strategies of survival and development / Andrei Kuznetsov editor
with the collaboration of Olav J. Sørensen.
p. cm.
Includes bibliographical references and index.
ISBN 0-7890-1417-3 (hard : alk. paper)–ISBN 0-7890-1418-1 (soft : alk. paper)
1. Corporations–Russia (Federation) 2. Industrial organization–Russia (Federation) 3. Industrial
management–Russia (Federation) 4. Finance–Russia (Federation) 5. Russia
(Federation)–Economic conditions–1991- I. Kuznetsov, A. I. (Andrei Igorevich). II.
Sørensen, Olav Jull. HD70.R9 R8625 2001
3338.7 4 094–dc21

2001051727

ISBN-13: 978-0-7890-1417-7 (hbk)
ISBN-13: 978-0-7890-1418-4 (pbk)
ISBN-13: 978-1-315-86503-4 (ebk)

Russian Corporations: The Strategies of Survival and Development

CONTENTS

ABOUT THE AUTHORS

Professor Sergei Aukutsionek is Head of the Centre for Research in Transition Economics at the Institute of World Economy and International Relations of the Russian Academy of Sciences, 23 Profsoyuznaya, GSP-7, Moscow; Russia (reb@avalon.ru)

Dr. Andrei Kuznetsov is Reader in International Business Management, Business School, the Manchester Metropolitan University, Aytoun Building, Aytoun Street, Manchester, M1 3GH UK (a.kuznetsov@mmu.ac.uk).

Dr. Olga Kuznetsova is Senior Research Fellow, Business School, the Manchester Metropolitan University, Aytoun Building, Aytoun Street, Manchester, M1 3GH UK (o.kuznetsova@mmu.ac.uk).

Professor Olav J. Sørensen, Centre for International Studies, the University of Aalborg. Fibigerstrede 2, 9220 Aalborg Ö, Denmark (OJS @i4.auc.dk).

Dr. Julia Popova is Head of the Department of Marketing and Statistics, Syktyvkar State University, 55 Oktiabrskij prosp., 167001, Syktyvkar, Russia (jfp@ssu.komitex.ru).

Dr. Rostislav Kapelyushnikov, the Institute of World Economy and International Relations of the Russian Academy of Sciences, 23 Profsoyuznaya, GSP-7, Moscow; Russia (reb@avalon.ru)

Alexandra Batyaeva, the Institute of World Economy and International Relations of the Russian Academy of Sciences, 23 Profsoyuznaya, GSP-7, Moscow; Russia (reb@avalon.ru)

ABOUT THE EDITOR

Andrei Kuznetsov, PhD, is Reader (Senior Associate Professor) in International Business at the Manchester Metropolitan University in the United Kingdom. His recent research in the area of business studies has been published in *Communist Economies & Economic Transformation, Europe-Asia Studies, Journal of East-West Business, Journal of Small Business Management, Russian and East European Finance and Trade* and other journals.

Introduction

Andrei Kuznetsov

Russia will be soon approaching the tenth anniversary of the launch of dramatic large-scale market reforms in the country. This has been an eventful period, but on balance, the results of the reforms were at best controversial. The expected rapid passage towards a functional market economy has largely failed to materialize. Consequently, there has been a noticeable drive towards the re-evaluation of the experience and outcomes of reforms in Russia. The major criticism is that "Washington Consensus" and the "shock therapy" approach to transformation were contemplated without due attention to the specific conditions of Russia (Stiglitz, 1999; Black, 1999; Hedlund, 2000). As a result the analysis of the realities and perspectives of the Russian economy and business environment was often marred by either applying unsubstantiated assumptions or ignoring some disturbing evidence that did not quite fit customary conceptions.

In the meantime, the Russian economy has acquired some intriguing characteristics that affect any firm or person wishing to do business in Russia. Most noticeable of them are the spread of barter transactions, low level of investment activities, labor hoarding, the importance of networks and unorthodox forms of corporate governance. These features have drawn much attention of western analysts who commonly evaluate them through the prism of western experience and mainstream western theories. No wonder those conclusions are usually not very favorable as far as the Russian business environment and its prospect are concerned. Yet, the features mentioned above have proved to be more than a passing mark of their time. More importantly these "irregularities" survived all attempts by the reformers to eliminate them and were still present

[Haworth co-indexing entry note]: "Introduction." Kuznetsov, Andrei. Co-published simultaneously in *Journal of East-West Business* (International Business Press, an imprint of The Haworth Press, Inc.) Vol. 6, No. 4, 2001, pp. 1-3; and: *Russian Corporations: The Strategies of Survival and Development* (ed: Andrei Kuznetsov) International Business Press, an imprint of The Haworth Press, Inc., 2001, pp. 1-3.

1

when the Russian economy finally showed some noticeable growth in the second quarter of 2000 for the first time in a decade.

The current volume comprises studies that seek to throw some new light on certain disputed aspects of the Russian business environment. They share a common approach, as the authors accept that the current situation in Russia is unique enough to restrain the chances of a successful application of most preconceptions unless they are appropriately modified first. With this in view, the authors concentrate on facts first and foremost. In this respect they enjoy a singular advantage of being able to use one of the best databases on Russian business development accumulated by the "The Russian Economic Barometer" (REB). REB, a research organization supported by the Russian Academy of Sciences, has been monitoring transitions to the market in Russia over seven years now using the results of monthly panel surveys of executive managers of hundreds of Russian firms.

The collection opens with the article by Batyaeva and Aukutsionek dealing with the little-known side of the Russian economic transition, the insufficient provision of capital investment. The article demonstrates that, contrary to common belief, there is no real crisis of capital investment in Russia as the ratio of capital accumulation in the country, although at a historical low by domestic standards, remains equal to most prosperous economies of the world. And yet, capital assets see hardly any modernization. The behavioral responses of Russian firms are investigated in order to find a solution to this paradox.

Barter has been recognized as one of the most notable peculiarities of the current business environment in Russia. Aukutsionek provides exhaustive evidence on the scale and scope of barter in the country. He claims that despite obvious negative consequences, the spread of barter in the 1990's made a crucial contribution towards the survival of the national industry in a meaningful form and will keep its prominence in the foreseeable future.

Barter is just one of the unusual features of the relations between buyers and sellers in modern Russia. Others include reliance on informal networks and rent seeking. Popova and Sørensen describe how Russian firms manage their relations with customers and suppliers under these conditions. They conclude that the Russian market is still very much the seller market and the August 1998 crisis has only reinforced this tendency following the devaluation of the ruble and a fall in demand for imports.

The evolvement of ownership structures and patterns of control in Russian firms is the focus of attention of Kapelyushnikov. He seeks to make a distinction between the largest and dominant shareholders in order to identify a link between the pattern of shareholding and the efficiency of firms. He establishes that companies with medium concentration of shareholdings are more successful than companies with dispersed or highly-concentrated ownership structure and firms under control of managers or financial outsiders outperform firms controlled by employees, non-financial outsiders or the state.

The paper by Kuznetsova and Kuznetsov evaluates the validity of the claim that insider shareholding is a major stumbling block on the way of enterprise restructuring in Russia. This paper argues in favor of a more balanced view, which takes into account the social responsibility of firms towards stake-holders and the influence the latter have over corporations' performance bounded by the transition environment.

REFERENCES

Black, B., Kraakman, K. and Tarassova, A. (1999). Russian Privatization and Corporate Governance: What Went Wrong? Working Paper 178. Stanford: Stanford Law School.

Hedlund, S. (1999). *Russia's "Market" Economy. A Bad Case of Predatory Capitalism.* London: UCL Press.

Stiglitz, J. (1999). Wither Reforms? Ten Years of the Transition. Keynote address at the Annual Conference of the World Bank on Development Economics, April 28-30, Washington.

Investment and Non-Investment in the Russian Industry

Alexandra Batyaeva
Sergei Aukutsionek

ABSTRACT. The dynamics of capital investment is a little-known aspect of the transitional crisis in Russia. On the one hand, it is undeniable that there was a drastic decline in capital investments in 1992-1998, which is often held responsible for the slow restructuring of the Russian industry. On the other hand, international comparisons show that in these years the ratio of capital accumulation in Russia was as high as in most prosperous economies. This paper studies the investment behavior of Russian firms in order to suggest possible explanations of this paradox. For this purpose it reveals and compares the characteristics of investing and non-investing firms and how these characteristics affect the efficiency of investment policy. Factors limiting capital investment are singled out, in particular those related to the sources of funds. *[Article copies available for a fee from The Haworth Document Delivery Service: 1-800-342-9678. E-mail address: <getinfo@haworthpressinc.com> Website: <http://www.HaworthPress.com> © 2001 by The Haworth Press, Inc. All rights reserved.]*

KEYWORDS. Industrial firm, investment, efficiency of investment, Russia

[Haworth co-indexing entry note]: "Investment and Non-Investment in the Russian Industry." Batyaeva, Alexandra, and Sergei Aukutsionek. Co-published simultaneously in *Journal of East-West Business* (International Business Press, an imprint of The Haworth Press, Inc.) Vol. 6, No. 4, 2001, pp. 5-22; and: *Russian Corporations: The Strategies of Survival and Development* (ed: Andrei Kuznetsov) International Business Press, an imprint of The Haworth Press, Inc., 2001, pp. 5-22.

Capital investments remain a poorly investigated area of transitional economics. This is not surprising, keeping in mind how difficult it is to measure investment activities in comparison with some other economic variables such as the level of prices, industrial output or employment. There is nothing obvious as far as investments are concerned. Even the most evident facts like the absolute decline of investment in Russian industry following the introduction of economic reforms in 1992 leave room for contradictory interpretations as soon as we try to make conclusions about the consequences of this phenomenon for the performance of Russian firms. In fact, the fixed investment ratio in Russia has been quite adequate by European standards at any time (Akutsionek and Batyaeva, 1997).

In this situation, it is extremely important to expand our factual knowledge about investment activities of Russian firms. The results of sample surveys should be seen as an important alternative source of data, complementing traditional statistics. This paper is based on the results of surveys conducted by the Russian Economic Barometer. These data will be used to expose the determinants affecting the behavior of Russian firms in the sphere of capital investment and possible prospects of their development.

COLLAPSE OF INVESTMENT ACTIVITIES

First of all, we will look at firms that do not invest. There are two main reasons for making them the central piece of this study. First, they make up a very substantial group of Russian firms, and therefore, are at least as representative as investing firms (Plakin, 1996).

The second reason is related to the difficulties of measuring capital investment activities at the micro-level. Even under normal conditions, capital investments of a company never represent a continuous flow (Pindyck, 1988). Rather, they exist in the form of a discretive process usually incorporating large periods of inactivity. This perception allows us to introduce a new indicator of investment activity in an industry: the share of firms that do not make any investments during a certain fixed period of time, for instance, two, six, or twelve months in succession. Following this approach, the non-uniform nature of capital investments receives an objective measurement.

REB has been collecting information on the investment activities of Russian industrial firms for several years now. The analysis of these data leaves no doubt that the phenomenon of non-investment spotted by some experts (Urinson, 1997) is indeed very widely spread in the Russian industry. On average, in 1993, more than a half of firms did not buy any equipment for two or more months in succession. By 1997 the share of such firms had grown to 65% of the total, and in 1998 it increased further to 70% of the total (Figure 1).

FIGURE 1. The Share of Firms Buying No Equipment for Two or More Months in Succession

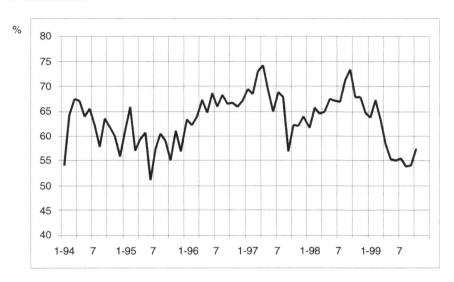

In reality, the actual period during which firms do not buy any equipment has been more than two months. In 1994-1998 it was about eight months on the average. One important observation that follows from REB surveys is that the share of actively-investing firms as well as the share of firms that do not invest is fairly stable over time. Thus, in 1994-1998, 33% of firms covered by REB surveys did not buy equipment at all, and only 2% bought it with any regularity (see Table 1). The remaining 65% of producers invested in equipment from time to time.

It is interesting to note that no direct correlation has been detected between the number of investing firms and the total decrease in the volume of sums spent by firms on capital investment. In 1993-1996, for example, the total volume of fixed capital investment in manufacturing fell by half. At the same time, the share of investing firms decreased only by a quarter. This means that the reduction of capital investment was distributed more or less evenly among those companies that were still investing. The same conclusion is suggested by the analysis of another similar indicator: the share of firms that made no capital investment, including construction investments, for six or more months in succession. In 1993-1996, the share of firms doing without any capital investment for half a year or longer rose from 25% to 44%. This means that the share of investing firms declined by no more than a quarter (from 75% to 56%).

TABLE 1. Distribution of Firms by the Length of the Period in Which They Did Not Buy Equipment, 1994-1998

Length of the period of non-investing		Share of firms
in months	% of total period of observation (1994-1998)	
60	100	33%
45-59	75-99	41%
30-44	50-74	18%
15-29	25-49	6%
0-14	0-24	2%

The finding that the decrease in investment has been spread rather evenly among investing firms leads to a possible explanation of why the share of investing and non-investing firms remains stable on the whole. We believe that, other things equal, the more even the distribution of contraction in investments is, the longer, on the average, firms remain part of the group of investors in which they had found themselves by the beginning of reforms. Indeed, as shown in Table 1, the period, during which firms stay in the non-investing group, is much longer than two or six months. Assessments of anticipated investment policy confirm this conclusion as may be seen from the typical data from the September 1997 survey. Among the firms that had not purchased any equipment for two and more months in succession, about 90% had no intention to buy any for at least another three months. Similarly, among those firms that had made no capital investments in six months prior to the survey, about 80% had no investment plans for the next half-year.

Clearly, the smaller the firm, the more irregular should be its flow of investments. While a giant factory is buying equipment every month, a small workshop will do this, probably, once every two years. How important is the size of the firm from the point of view of its propensity to invest? Would it be correct to assume that smaller firms are more likely to enter the non-investing group?

Indeed, the difference in the size of firms between the two groups is quite substantial. Survey after survey, the number of employees in firms belonging to the investing group was 1.5-2 times larger than the same indicator for the non-investing group (see Table 2). However, this difference in size is not substantial enough to explain fully or even partly the observed variance of investment activities. This is obvious from the following data. During three years (1995-1997), the average number of employees in firms of both groups declined approximately by a third. As a result, in 1997 the size of investing firms in terms of employee numbers (and respectively, the scope of their business activity) had become almost equal to the size of non-investing firms of 1995. However, if the hypothesis that the size of business is a prevailing factor in de-

TABLE 2. Average Number of Employees at Non-Investing and Investing Firms During Six Months Before the Survey

Groups of firms	1995	1996	1997 Jan.-Sept.	1997/1996, %
Non-investing firms	673	613	466	69%
Investing firms	1210	975	817	68%

termining the investment behavior of firms were true, *the average size of investing firms would most probably remain unchanged or, at least, would not decline so sharply.*

Finally, REB surveys allow one to find out how the firms of these two groups are distributed by the sector of manufacturing. As follows from Table 3, over the period of observations, firms manufacturing investment products were the least keen on making capital investments.

INVESTING VERSUS NON-INVESTING FIRMS

What types of firms invest? "The more successful ones" should probably be the most general answer. Success may be measured in relative terms using a number of parameters. One of them is *the rate of capacity utilization.* In 1995-1996, this rate was 12-14% higher in the group of investing firms than in the group of non-investing firms. In 1997, this gap narrowed somewhat, but it was still quite noticeable (see Table 4). The difference in terms of *received orders* is another possible measure. Here, the cleft between investing and non-investing firms has been also significant and stable. Both indicators demonstrate that investing firms have adapted themselves to the conditions of demand much better.

Superior *financial performance* of investing firms may be regarded as a consequence of this adaptation. As shown in Table 4, among investing firms, the share of financially successful (i.e., those that assess their financial condition as "good" or "normal") is about three times as high as in the group of non-investing firms. Finally, investing firms have an enduring and significant edge in terms of the average levels of *wages.* These levels have been up to a third higher than in the firms of the non-investing group.

The link between investing and the performance of firms becomes quite obvious when cross-industry figures are compared (see Table 5 and Figure 2). The share of investing firms is relatively high in such sectors as food, electric power, and metals, which are coping quite well with transition. This share is low in light industry and engineering, the two most affected sectors.

TABLE 3. Share of Non-Investing Firms by Sector of Manufacturing (%)

Sectors of manufacturing	1994	1995	1996	Jan.-Sept. 1997
Not buying equipment for two and more months in succession				
Consumer goods	65	62	63	58
Capital goods	72	67	74	76
Producers' goods	54	51	60	63
Not making capital investments for six and more months				
Consumer goods	31	40	43	38
Capital goods	36	49	53	50
Producers' goods	32	29	40	38

TABLE 4. Business Indicators of Investing and Non-Investing Firms During Six Months Before the Survey

	1995	1996	1997 Jan.-Sept.
Capacity utilization rate (normal level = 100)			
Non-investing firms	52	47	49
Investing firms	64	61	58
Received orders (normal level = 100)			
Non-investing firms	64	57	56
Investing firms	75	69	68
Share of financially successful firms (% of the number of firms in each group)			
Non-investing firms	13	8	11
Investing firms	38	23	32
Relative wages per employee (wages in the investing group = 100)			
Non-investing firms	71	75	75
Investing firms	100	100	100

The distorted system of payment settlements between suppliers and buyers, causing substantial delays in financial transfers between companies, is often referred to as the main reason of the low investment activity of Russian industrial firms. REB data, however, do not support this assumption. Judging by the percentage of barter in sales and the share of cash settlements in both groups of firms (see Table 6), the claim that the investment activity of firms is influenced by the state of financial settlements receives no confirmation. Both investing and non-investing firms have approximately the same pattern of payment settlements. In 1994-1998, the percentage of barter, on the average, was equal to about 1/3 of sales for each category of firms, and the share of cash settlements to about 1/8-1/7.

TABLE 5. Comparison of Shares of Investing and Financially Successful Firms by Industry, 1994-1998 (%)

	Share of investing* firms	Share of financially successful firms
Light industry	29	19
Machinery	46	16
Lumber, pulp and paper	46	15
Fuel industries	50	11
Chemicals and petrochemicals	60	24
Construction materials	54	16
Foods	69	20
Metals	77	23
Electric power	63	41

*Investing are those firms that made investments within a half of a year

FIGURE 2. Comparison of Shares of Investing and Financially Successful Firms by Industry, 1994-1998, %

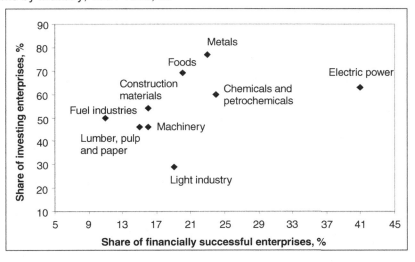

DO LESS PROFITABLE FIRMS ACTUALLY INVEST LESS?

The data examined in the previous section present some evidence that more successful businesses are responsible for the lion's share of capital investment in Russia. Yet, the indicators that were used in our analysis provide only an indirect assessment of the performance of the firm. Therefore, in this section we

TABLE 6. Methods of Payment Settlement Used by Investing and Non-Investing Firms

	Non-investing firms	Investing firms
Share of barter (average, 1994-1998), %	31	33
Share of barter (1998), %	50	49
Share of cash settlements (average, 1997-1998), %	12	15

will look at some variables directly related to the profit-earning capacity of the firms. The question we will try to find an answer to is the following: Is it true that profit-making firms invest more than loss-making ones?

Data in Table 7, we believe, give conclusive evidence essential to answer this question. In 1994-1998, on the average, no more than one out of five loss-making firms purchased equipment at least once every two months. At the same time, almost half of profit-makers invested regularly. Firms that just managed to match their income and costs occupy an intermediate position between loss-makers and profit-makers: one out of three firms in such position was a regular investor.

There is one other indicator of profitability employed by REB studies. It is *the highest interest rate on bank loans that the firm can afford to finance its capital investment for the period of two or three years.* Let us call this indicator a *marginal credit rate* (MCR). It is a speculative criterion as compared with indicators of actual profitability. At the same time it allows to analyze firm performance over a longer period of time and it is better fit to explore the correlation between profitability and ability of the firm to invest (Metcalf and Hassett, 1995).

This marginal credit rate (MCR) was falling at a steady pace as inflation was slowing down in the years preceding the crisis of August 1998. While in May 1996 MCR was 33%, it fell down to 8% by August 1997. It is clear that, other factors being equal, MCR is determined by the *anticipated return on investment* peculiar to every firm. The higher the expected return on an investment project is, the more the firm can afford to pay for a credit to finance this project. Therefore, it makes sense to divide the sample of surveyed firms into two groups by the level of MCR. The first group will include firms with high expected return on investment as denoted by higher than average MCR. The second group consists of firms with low expected return on investment as indicated by lower than the average MCR.

As may be concluded from the data presented in Table 8, this test also gives a positive result in the sense that non-investing firms may be found only rarely among firms with high expected returns on investment. It is true though that

TABLE 7. Purchases of Equipment and Indicators of Profitability

	1994	1995	1996	1997 Jan.-Sept.	Average
Share of firms not buying equipment for two and more months in succession					
Profits	58	49	52	54	53
Balance (income = costs)	58	61	70	69	64
Losses	75	79	79	86	80
Share of firms not going to buy equipment in the next three months					
Profits	54	42	49	46	48
Balance (income = costs)	56	56	63	64	60
Losses	78	74	73	81	76

TABLE 8. Purchases of Equipment and Marginal Credit Rates (MCR) of Firms with High and Low Expected Return on Investment

Groups of firms by level of expected return on investment (MCR)	1996 May	1996 Aug.	1996 Nov.	1997 Feb.	1997 May	1997 Aug.
Share of firms not buying equipment for two and more months in succession, %						
High expected return on investment	54	57	58	64	70	65
Low expected return on investment	65	69	73	74	73	70
Share of firms not going to buy equipment in the next three months, %						
High expected return on investment	57	50	58	62	60	63
Low expected return on investment	61	70	74	71	72	67
Marginal credit rates, %						
High expected return on investment	85	41	25	25	12	14
Low expected return on investment	25	9	5	5	3	4
Total sample	33	21	15	14	8	8

following this method, the difference between the two groups is less significant than if we used as a criterion the six-month profit rate. In May and August 1997, the disparity was as small as 3-5 percentage points. This may be the sign of a significant closing of the gap between MCR values for the two groups of firms at that moment. While in 1996 this gap could be measured in two-digit numbers, by August 1997, it was not wider than 9-10 percentage points.

Comparing the data presented in Tables 7 and 8, it is possible to make the conclusion that the expected return on investment is by far less significant in determining the scope and regularity of investment activity of firms than such parameters as current profits and losses. Moreover, taking into account the rate of inflation (about 10-12 per cent in 1997), we may deduce that firms in the low-profitable group could afford only loans with negative real interest rates. Put differently, the data confirm that *a large portion of investment by Russian firms is made without the anticipation of any returns at all.*

EFFICIENCY OF INVESTMENT ACTIVITY

It is important to be able to identify the connection between the financial standing of the firm and its investment activity as it reveals itself in the modern Russian business environment (Balatskii, 1996). Statistics collected by REB give a rare opportunity to explore this problem, tracing the activities of investing firms during a substantial period of time (up to two years). Since the level of investment activity in the country has been generally low, it is clear that the number of firms that consistently invested over such a period should be relatively small. In the REB sample, there happened to be 88 firms that were investing over twelve months in a succession, of which just 34 continued to invest over 24 months (the observation refers to 1996-1998). Surveys provide information about their self-assessment of their own financial condition on the scale of good–normal–poor, and responses about their performance by half-year periods (profit–balance–loss). In the latter case, respondents indicated whether their firm achieved profits, a break-even point or had losses. For the purpose of our study, we have to compare changes in both assessments over the period of observation.

As seen from Table 9, relatively long (by crisis standards) investment activity of producers allows them at least to retain their competitive positions: 56% of firms having invested for one year, and 59% of those having done so for two years had their financial indicators unchanged. Since, overall, there are more profit-makers and financially successful firms among investing firms, we can conclude that investment activity generally helps firms to maintain better positions within their peer group.

At the same time, in about a quarter of all cases, investing has resulted in a deteriorating financial position. Moreover, this tendency can be seen more distinctly within a longer time range. The financial position got poorer in 23% of those firms that invested during one year, and in 26% of those that did so for

TABLE 9. Financial Indicators of Investing Firms (End of the Investing Period, as Compared with Its Beginning)

Financial indicators	Firms investing for	
	One year, %	two years, %
Deteriorated	23	26
Remained unchanged	56	59
Improved	21	15
	100%	100%
Number of firms	88	34

two years. Across the sample, the share of firms with improved financial condition declined on the whole from 21% to 15%.

This data suggest that in 56-59% of all cases, investment activity helps Russian industrial firms to keep their financial condition relatively healthy. In 15-22% of cases, investing firms even improve their financial standing. However, in 23-26% of cases, investments did not prevent some deterioration of this standing. In other words, investment activities have been largely inefficient. This is an indirect confirmation of the hypothesis that we proposed earlier, i.e., that in Russian conditions, the decision by a firm to invest may reflect considerations other than increasing profit.

FACTORS LIMITING CAPITAL INVESTMENT

According to REB surveys, as a rule, top managers see no particular problems regarding returns on investments made by their firms (see also Zubakin, 1994). In 1997, on the average, no more than seven percent of REB respondents reported that their investment activities were limited by insufficient rates of return on investment projects. Interestingly, the deepening of the economic crisis did not result in any increase in this average. In the recent years, however, from 2/3 to 3/4 of all responding managers point to the lack of financial funds as the major limitation of capital investment.

In the situation of the acute shortage of financial resources, according to theory at least, firms should rely first and foremost on bank credits. However, in Russia, a substantial part of industrial firms have nearly exhausted their credit potentials (see Table 10). The share of such firms had been growing steadily from 22% in 1993 to 40% in 1997. In other words, an investment boom has not yet started, but the accumulated debt of firms is already so high that, as many managers believe, firms now are prevented from taking new credits to finance capital investment.

This *excessive indebtedness* is particularly distressing because it is developing against the background of a continuous decline of lending rates, making them of less importance as a factor limiting investment activities of businesses. For example, while in 1996 the share of respondents that mentioned lending rates as an important obstruction was between 30 and 40%, in 1997-1998 it dipped to 22-24%.

Investing and non-investing firms look from somewhat different angles at existing limitations on investment. Investing firms complain more frequently about low returns on their investments (8% of investing firms against 5% of non-investing ones) (Table 11). Similarly, more investing firms than non-in-

TABLE 10. Major Factors Limiting Capital Investment (Share of Firm Managers Having Pointed Out Each Factor, %)*

	1993	1994	1995	1996	1997	1998
1. Lack of financial funds	74	63	69	71	73	81
2. High prices of equipment	69	57	59	50	50	46
3. High indebtedness	22	31	36	37	40	38
4. High borrowing rate	32	39	31	28	22	24
5. Excessive production capacities	6	12	14	16	20	16
6. Insufficient rate of return on investment projects	-	8	6	6	7	4

* Respondents were offered to choose no more than three items from ten factors set out in the questionnaire.

TABLE 11. Major Factors Limiting Investment: Share of Managers Having Pointed Out Every Factor (%)*

	1994	1995	1996	1997	1998	Average
Lack of financial funds						
Non-investing firms	51	66	65	72	76	65
Investing firms	68	70	76	78	79	74
High prices of equipment and construction works						
Non-investing firms	52	59	48	47	40	50
Investing firms	64	64	56	56	48	58
High level of debt						
Non-investing firms	31	41	42	48	54	42
Investing firms	34	36	35	40	34	36
High interest on borrowings						
Non-investing firms	41	35	29	22	28	31
Investing firms	42	32	30	24	28	32
Surplus of production capacities						
Non-investing firms	17	18	21	22	18	19
Investing firms	11	14	15	20	16	15
Insufficient return on investment projects						
Non-investing firms	7	5	5	7	3	5
Investing firms	9	9	9	9	6	8

* Respondents were offered to choose no more than three items from the factors set out in the questionnaire.

vesting firms are concerned with lack of financial funds and too high prices of equipment and construction works.

As a matter of fact, these differences are easy to explain. "Zero investments" require no financing and are sensitive neither to prices nor to rates of return. But there are certain problems to which non-investing firms are exposed to more frequently. The first is the larger surplus of production capacities (19% counter 15% in investing firms), and the second is their higher level of debt (42% against 36%). Moreover, the difference between the two groups in terms of debt level is growing steadily, which is reflected in the fact that in 1998, this problem was quoted by 54% of all non-investing firms against 34% of the investing ones.

SOURCES OF FUNDS FOR CAPITAL INVESTMENT

Considering the importance of the lack of funds as a factor hindering investment by industrial firms, it is important to find out what sources of funds are available to these firms (Vitin 1994, 1996, 1998; Astapovich and Grigoriec 1993; Samuelson 1993). To a certain point, Table 12 contains the answer to this question. It shows the classification of the main possible sources of investment funds as ranked by firm managers. Some aspects of the opinions expressed by respondents and summarized in this table are worth attention.

First, by the late 1998, there had been a noticeable decline in the degree of pessimism demonstrated by respondents in regard of the availability of access to investment funds, despite the fact that 40% of all surveyed managers still believed that they would not be able to raise any funds at all to invest in the next two or three years. Second, there was a growing number of firms inclined to increase self-financing using internal resources. Finally, the share of managers still hoping to borrow the money from banks plunged from 16% in 1997, the highest proportion over the whole period of surveying, to only 8% in 1998. As far as other channels of financing are concerned, such as aid from the government, domestic or foreign partners, or proceedings from selling shares, their expected role in financing the forthcoming investment boom looks quite insignificant (no more than 9%). And there is no sign of expectations that their role is going to grow.

Assessments of the most possible sources of funds differ by industry (Table 13). Managers of firms in the light industry expressed the strongest pessimism: over a half of them had no hope to find any funds to invest in the next two or three years. In power generation, fuel and food industries, managers relied on firms' own savings to the greatest extent: from 1/4 to 1/3 of them hoped to invest from internal sources. Bank credits were chosen as the most probable sources of funds for capital investment by respondents in such industries as food, chemicals and petrochemicals, and electric power. Nevertheless, even in these cases, only 1 firm in 5 picked banks.

In conclusion, let us compare the expectations of investing and non-investing firms in respect of possible sources of investment funds (Table 14). The largest variance is seen between pessimists in both groups. On average just

TABLE 12. Sources of Investment Funds in the Next Two or Three Years: Share of Respondents Who Selected Each Source as the Most Plausible (%)*

	Nov. 1996	May 1997	Nov. 1997	May 1998	Nov. 1998
1. Funds will come from nowhere	49	46	36	49	40
2. The firm will make savings	18	21	24	21	33
3. Borrowings from commercial banks	13	14	16	13	8
4. From a domestic partner	7	9	9	9	7
5. From a foreign partner	7	6	9	7	7
6. From the sale of shares	5	4	6	4	3
7. From the government	9	8	6	8	7
8. Other sources	2	17	4	4	6
9. Hard to answer	19	20	18	21	15

* Respondents were offered to choose no more than two versions of answer.

TABLE 13. Sources of Investment Funds in the Next Two or Three Years: Share of Respondents (%) Choosing a Particular Source as the Most Plausible, 1996-1997

Electric power	Fuel	Metals	Machinery	Chemicals and petro-chemicals	Lumber, pulp and paper	Construction materials	Light industry	Food	Others
No accessible sources									
36	31	27	48	23	38	47	56	41	47
The firm will make savings									
33	25	12	21	3	14	24	21	27	18
Borrowings from commercial banks									
19	10	7	16	20	5	16	12	21	7
Domestic or foreign partner									
0	6	17	15	20	25	25	9	14	17
The sale of shares									
28	4	0	5	0	4	7	1	5	7
The government									
6	7	14	6	13	9	2	13	5	27

over 43% of the managers of investing firms believed that they would never find any funds. In the other group such opinion was expressed by about 2/3 of all respondents. Another significant difference has to do with the views of managers on self-financing. In the investing group, over a third of respondents thought they would be able to tap this source of funds, while only slightly over 10% of respondents held this view in the non-investing group. There are not

TABLE 14. Sources of Investment Funds in the Next Two or Three Years: Share of Respondents (%) Choosing a Particular Source as the Most Plausible*

	Nov. '96	May '97	Nov. '97	May '98	Nov. '98	1996-1998
No accessible sources						
Non-investing firms	66	59	57	61	51	59
Investing firms	36	39	30	40	29	35
Aid from the government						
Non-investing firms	7	6	7	10	10	8
Investing firms	13	9	5	8	5	8
Borrowings from commercial banks						
Non-investing firms	3	9	14	10	7	9
Investing firms	24	17	20	19	10	18
The firm will make savings						
Non-investing firms	6	15	13	9	20	13
Investing firms	31	32	36	37	46	36
The sale of shares						
Non-investing firms	3	2	6	2	2	3
Investing firms	8	6	8	6	4	6
Domestic or a foreign partner						
Non-investing firms	6	15	8	7	10	7
Investing firms	8	6	8	6	4	6
Hard to answer						
Non-investing firms	22	25	22	23	22	23
Investing firms	21	24	23	27	22	23

* Respondents were offered to choose no more than two versions of answer.

only differences between the two groups. Managers across the board had no faith in such sources of funds as support from the government, domestic or foreign partners. Raising finance by selling shares was also generally mistrusted.

PARTICIPATION OF BANKS IN THE INVESTMENT ACTIVITIES OF FIRMS

REB studies of business ties between Russian banks and industrial firms suggest that, until recently, banks failed in their function of channeling available financial resources to the most efficient businesses. This follows from the fact that, paradoxically, the most successful firms remain in isolation as far as the banking sector is concerned. Indeed, although banks appear to charge identical rates on credits to both investing and non-investing firms, non-investing firms seem to have a more ready access to bank coffers than investing firms (Table 15). Moreover, as time goes by, investing firms have to face the diffi-

TABLE 15. Business Ties Between Banks and Industrial Firms

	1994	1995	1996	1997	1998	Average
Indebtedness to banks, % of a normal level						
Non-investing firms	-	-	139	137	122	135
Investing firms	-	-	111	90	78	96
Cost of borrowings, % a year						
Non-investing firms	169	145	97	33	26	101
Investing firms	175	147	96	33	30	103
Share of firms using no bank credits for three and more months in succession, %						
Non-investing firms	28	26	35	42	49	33
Investing firms	20	28	28	32	36	27

culty of getting bank credits mounting. Between 1996 and 1998, their debt to banks has declined by 33%, falling almost a quarter below its desirable level.

Recent surveys by REB reflect some change in the attitude of banks towards their industrial clients. Currently, the number of banks among REB respondents that regard lending to industrial firms as attractive business is larger than the number of those who still believe that such operations are unprofitable. However, it should be remembered that advances to industrial firms are still usually not higher than 25-35% of total lending portfolios of banks, and there are no signs that this share has been growing. To reflect this new interest of banks in industrial firms, REB sought the opinion of bankers on the profitability of various industries (See Table 16. Note that the data for October 1998 are not averaged with previous surveys to account for changes in the ranking of industries after August 1998 crisis).

Prior to August 1998, firms in the fuel and food industries were the most attractive in the eyes of banks in terms of long-term lending. The distant second were such industries as chemicals, machinery, and metals. The August crisis has changed the situation quite dramatically. First, the number of banks believing that all industries are a bad choice declined from 22% to 15%. Second, firms in the food industry have improved further their rating in the credit market. The relatively high rating of electric power remained virtually unchanged, while engineering and the light industry failed to improve their positions.

As it was already noted in this paper, the investment activity of industrial firms is largely determined by demand for their products. In this connection, it is interesting to find out whether priorities of banks in lending to industrial firms (as they are revealed in REB surveys) are consistent with the condition of demand in certain industries. As the results of our calculations show (Table 16), there is a correlation. Light industry and engineering are ranked low because of the poor state of their order-books; metals, chemicals, petrochemicals and fuel incite little interest in banks as well, because the demand for their

TABLE 16. Credit Rating by industry: Share of Banks That Chose a Particular Industry as the Best Choice for Investment Credit (%)

	Averaged estimates of credit rating		Order-books, % of the normal level		
	calculated from the data				
	of REB bank sample		of REB industrial sample		
	July 1997-June 1998	October 1998	July 1997-June 1998	Aug. 1998-Dec. 1998	
	(1)	(2)	(3)	(4)	(5) = (4)−(3)
Food	37	61	66	74	+8
Electric power	30	28	93	82	−11
Construction materials	11	17	60	69	+9
Lumber, pulp and paper	6	17	77	78	+1
Fuel	28	17	71	68	−3
Chemicals and petrochemicals	11	11	75	70	−5
Metals	11	11	81	76	−5
Machinery	6	6	57	57	0
Light industry	6	6	58	63	+5
All industries are bad	22	15	−	−	−

products is poor or declining. Consequently, the upper four positions are occupied by the industries that are enjoying high or growing demand–food, electrical power generation, construction materials, lumber, pulp and paper.

This analysis has demonstrated that despite a relatively high fixed investment ratio typical of the Russian economy, regular capital investment is still the prerogative of the absolute minority of industrial firms. About two thirds of industrial firms do not buy any equipment for periods as long as half a year, and a third make no capital investment for the period of a year. Lack of financial funds is the biggest barrier to their investment activity. The role of profits as an incentive to long-term investing is negligibly small. Over a third of all firms have no hope to find any sources of funds to invest and are skeptical about getting credits from banks. However, there is a positive tendency that a growing number of firms are relying on internal resources as a source of capital investment.

REFERENCES

Astapovich, A. and Grigoriev, L. (1993). Inostrannye investitsii v Rossii: problemy i resheniya. *MEMO*, 5, 16-29

Aukutsionek, S. and Batyaeva A. (1997). Investment in Russian Industry. *Russian Economic Barometer*, (VI)4, 3-13.

Balatskii, E. (1996) Effektivnost' investitsii v otkrytoi ekonomike, mirovaya ekonomika i mezhdunarodnye otnosheniya. *MEMO,* 10, 40-49

Metcalf, G. E. and Hassett, K.A. (1995) Investment under Alternative Return Assumptions. Comparing Random Walks and Mean Reversion. *Journal of Economic Dynamics and Control,* 19, 1471-1488

Pindyck, R.S. (1988). Irreversible Investment, Capacity Choice, and the Value of the Firm. *American Economic Review,* 78, 969-985.

Plakin, V. (1996). Krizis investitsionnoi sfery rossiiskoi ekonomiki i puti ego preodoleniya. *Voprosy ekonomiki,* 12, 101-111.

Samuelson, G.-F. (1993). Pryamye zarubezhnye investitsii v ramkakh novoi paradigmy razvitiya dlya respublik byvshego Sovetskogo Souyza. *Voprosy ekonomiki,* 3, 70-77.

Urinson, Y. (1997). O merakh po ozhivleniyu investitsionnogo protsessa v Rossii. *Voprosy ekonomiki,* 1, 69-76.

Vitin, A. (1994). Mobilizatsiya finansovikh resursov dlya investitsii. *Voprosy ekonomiki,* 7, 13-21.

Vitin, A. (1996). "Privlechenie investitsii na rynke tsennykh bumag. *Voprosy ekonomiki,* 12, 121-128.

Vitin, A. (1998). Rynok tsennykh bumag i investitsii: krizis i predposylki ego preodoleniya. *Voprosy ekonomiki,* 9, 136-147.

Zubakin, V. (1994). Investitsii v privatizirovannye predpriiatia. *Voprosy ekonomiki,* 7, 22-30.

SUBMITTED: September 1999
FIRST REVISION: January 2000
SECOND REVISION: March 2000
ACCEPTED: August 2000

Barter:
New Data and Comments

Sergei Aukutsionek

ABSTRACT. Barter transactions have reached an unprecedented scale in the modern Russian economy. Practically all industrial firms are involved in barter and for many of them, barter represents as much as half or more of their entire turnover. This phenomenon cannot be appraised in simplified terms. Its role is contradictory. There is no doubt that it has serious negative consequences as far as the success of market reforms is concerned. However, this paper argues that barter has helped the Russian economy to survive in the critical years of post-communist transition. *[Article copies available for a fee from The Haworth Document Delivery Service: 1-800-342-9678. E-mail address: <getinfo@haworthpressinc.com> Website: <http://www.HaworthPress.com> © 2001 by The Haworth Press, Inc. All rights reserved.]*

KEYWORDS. Barter, industrial firms, transitional economy

INTRODUCTION

Traditionally, economic theory has considered barter transactions as a less efficient and dated form of trade compared to money transactions. It is the universal recognition attribute of money that makes it superior to commodity money. Furthermore, according to Williamson and Wright (1994), the use of money encourages exchange of high-quality products and requires less time

---

[Haworth co-indexing entry note]: "Barter: New Data and Comments." Aukutsionek, Sergei. Co-published simultaneously in *Journal of East-West Business* (International Business Press, an imprint of The Haworth Press, Inc.) Vol. 6, No. 4, 2001, pp. 23-35; and: *Russian Corporations: The Strategies of Survival and Development* (ed: Andrei Kuznetsov) International Business Press, an imprint of The Haworth Press, Inc., 2001, pp. 23-35.

to complete the transaction. Overall, reported business practices confirm the theory. One of the studies (Neale et al., 1992) identified only a very small number of the leading firms in the UK and Canada engaged in domestic countertrade, with the main motivations for participation being the desire to administer hidden price discounting and to circumvent short-term credit shortages.

The most important deterrent to barter transactions is the cost of gathering information about the characteristics and attributes of goods available for exchange (Alchian, 1977). Nonetheless, in the last 25 years, there has been a noticeable increase in the level of barter activities in market economies. In the United States, the number of firms regularly involved in barter transactions has risen 23 times from 17,000 to 400,000 during the 1976 to 1996 period (Marvasti and Smyth, 1999). This growth has become possible as a result of the emergence of a new form of barter facilitated by specialized barter exchanges that have reduced the information inefficiency of barter trade. Outside the US barter exchanges, profit-seeking organizations that generate income by charging fees and commissions, operate in Australia, Canada, New Zealand and the UK. Membership brings such benefits as access to new customers, increased sales and networking opportunities.

The spread of business-to-business barter indicates that this form of exchange may coexist with a money-based market economy and even supplement it. Yet, despite a spectacular growth, barter trade has a long way to go before it may start playing any significant role. It is still mostly limited to very small companies and even for the members of barter exchanges, this type of transaction contributes only a fraction of their annual gross sales (for instance, according to Birxh and Liesch (1998), just 5% in the case of Australia).

Barter is not limited to mature market economies. Actually, widespread barter has been one of the most striking and original features of the Russian economy in recent years. With no obvious reason, an enormous system of decentralised exchange in kind spontaneously emerged in the Russian industry in the wake of the market reforms. This system is very different from its western counterpart in many important instances. It is not institutionalized and is not built around barter exchanges. At the same time, in terms of turnover, it is possibly the largest in the entire human history. For many Russian firms, including the largest, barter has become the main form of trade, responsible for as much as 73% of their business.

Currently, it is quite impossible to foresee how long this system is going to exist. It may be decades or just years, as there is some evidence that barter has been shrinking since the late 1998. It has already attracted much attention on the part of Western experts. Its existence is mostly seen as a source of significant negative consequences, the main being that it hinders enterprise restructuring and measuring economic performance (Gaddy and Ickes 1998). In this paper, we will try to evaluate the role of barter in the modern Russian economy using the results of surveys of Russian managers. This will allow us to give a more balanced interpretation of this phenomenon in the context of the turbulent Russian business environment.

DYNAMICS OF BARTER IN 1992-1999

There was a number of attempts to measure the degree of barterization of the Russian industry resulting in a variety of estimates. This analysis is based on statistics extracted from the surveys carried out by REB, an independent research center based in Moscow. The unique strength of this database is that it is probably the only source of *regular and systematic* information describing the share of barter exchange in the Russian industry since 1992. There is also a weakness connected to a relatively small size of the sample group. Normally only from 150 to 200 firms are surveyed every month. However, every care is taken to make this sample representative. Its composition reflects all main features of the Russian industrial sector in terms of distribution by industry, region, size and the form of ownership.

Another feature of REB statistics is that total figures are calculated with no regard to the difference in the size of enterprises. In this context, the share of barter in sales represents an average per enterprise rather than an average per unit of output in industry as a whole. However, this feature of REB statistics does not make much difference in terms of qualitative analysis. As special additional research demonstrates, if the size differentiation of enterprises is taken into consideration, the share of barter transactions goes up for no more than 5-8 percentage points.

For the purpose of this study, total industrial output in Russia (Q) may be divided into the barter component (B), i.e., the share of output distributed through barter, and the non-barter component (N), i.e., the share of output distributed through normal market channels. If we ignore the relatively small part of output hoarded by producers in the form of inventories, then

$$Q = B + N \tag{1}$$

Primary data captured by REB surveys reveal *the percentage of output for barter* based on the formulae $100 \times (B{:}Q)$. In seven years of observation, this percentage grew 8.5 times from 6% in 1992 to 51% in 1998. Not in a single survey was it equal to zero. Its lowest relative level was registered in April-

June 1992 at 4-5% of total sales. The highest level was registered in August 1998 at 54%.

The dynamics of barter in 1998 deserves special attention. In August 1998, a severe financial crisis struck Russia, resulting in a fourfold devaluation of the national currency, a surge in domestic prices and a decline in the consumption of imported goods. Meanwhile, the banking system in the country was virtually paralyzed for several months as payments were "clogged" and deposits were blocked on the accounts. It is at this moment of a dramatic shortage of liquidity felt all over the country that the long-term trend in barter trade made an inverted U-turn, indicating a change from many years of growth to many months of decline.

This was a very significant development. As yet, it is difficult to fully foresee the possible implications this inverted U-turn for Russian firms. Two scenarios are plausible. This may be a beginning of the end of barter trade in Russia. Alternatively, barter transactions are going to reach a new equilibrium level that will become a pivotal point for further fluctuations. Indeed, the first option is preferable from the point of view of the success of market reforms. However, this outcome would be only possible if a wide range of conditions affecting Russian firms were normalized first. At present, it appears that Russian firms have passed the peak of their dependence on barter. They are trying now to achieve some equilibrium in the structure of their sales, which appears to lay within the range of 30-50% of total sales, pending important changes in the operational environment. Another interesting feature of Russian trading may be noted. Whenever barter transactions have been replaced with sales for cash, these take the form that excluded any participation on the part of banks. Thus, since August 1998 till May 1999, the share of barter transactions declined by 10 percentage points from 54% to 44%, which was roughly equal to the increase by 9 percentage points (from 15% to 24%) in what may be called over-the-counter sales.

The primary data presented so far do not give an adequate picture of the real scale of barterization because they do not account either for the absolute volume of output for barter or for its rate of growth. Theoretically, the replacement of one form of exchange with another may happen under various macro conditions, such as economic crisis or recovery. Equally, this replacement may be accompanied by a change in the volumes of B and N so that both components grow/decrease together or one component grows while the other declines. The actual pattern revealed by REB surveys in 1992-1998 was characterized by a decrease in total output Q and even a more rapid decrease in its non-barter component, N, contrasted by a rapid growth of output for barter in *absolute* terms.

The rate of this growth was remarkably high. In just six years from 1992 the absolute volume of output for barter by Russian industrial firms expanded 5.6 times at an impressive average rate of 33% a year. During the same period, total output decreased by more that 1/3 at the annual rate of 7% and the volume of non-barter output shrunk even further by more than 2/3 (a fall of 17% a year (see Table 1)).

THE MEASUREMENT OF BARTER BY INDUSTRY

As the current round of market reforms started in 1992, all industries had practically the same level of barter transactions. The gap between industries with the highest share of barter and those with the lowest share was no more than 8-10 percentage points. By 1997-98, this gap had expanded more than 3 times, so that "leaders" in barterization were ahead of industries with minimal barter turnover by 34-37 percentage points. During seven years covered by REB surveys, construction materials and metals emerged as demonstrating consistently the highest levels of barter. And the two industries with the lowest levels of barterization were food and fuel industry.

These statistics, however, do not fully display the situation with barter by industry because they do not account for changes in the *absolute volumes* of output for barter. As a matter of fact, in 1992-1997, there was no decline in the absolute volume of output for barter in any single industry despite the fact that the degree of barterization across industries was irregular and total output declined dramatically. Fuel industry topped the list, demonstrating the record sevenfold growth of output for barter in 1992-1997. Light industry came last,

TABLE 1. Dynamics of Barter in the Russian Industry, 1992-1998 (Annual Figures, Average for 12 months, %)

Year	Share of barter in sales	Increase in the share (percentage points)	Index of barter output (at constant prices)	Growth rate of barter output	Index of non-barter output (at constant prices)
1992	6*)	−	100	−	100
1993	9	+3	131	+31	83
1994	17	+8	206	+57	60
1995	22	+5	251	+22	55
1996	35	+13	384	+53	44
1997	42	+7	499	+30	38
1998	51	+9	564	+13	33

*) Average for February - December
Sources: Calculated from Goskomstat data and REB Survey statistics

lagging far behind all other industries with "only" a two-fold growth of its output for barter (see Table 2).

Interestingly, there was a noticeable difference between the ranking of industries by the rate of absolute increase of output for barter comparing to the ranking by the share of barter transactions in sales. It is well known that light industry in Russia was among the most seriously affected by the transitional crisis. Within five years since 1992 to 1997, its output (Q) declined almost by 80%. However, against this background of general decline, the absolute volume of barter output (B) was growing really fast by 16% a year. Overall, industries that were oriented towards effective demand (N) suffered the most severe contraction. The average annual decrease of 9% in non-barter output was registered even in energy production, an industry that was in the most favorable situation comparing to all other producers because of secure demand in export markets. As for light industry, its average annual rate of decrease in N was 35%.

It is instructive to look at the relative importance of the various methods of selling used by industrial firms in Russia. For this purpose the non-barter output N has to be divided further into sales for cash (C) and the other sales (R):

$$Q = B + N = B + C + R \qquad (2)$$

As could be expected, some industries rely on barter more than others (Table 3). The manufacturers of investment goods use barter the most. Although the conventional division of industries into the producers of investment goods and

TABLE 2. Dynamics of Barter by Industries

	Share of barter in sales, 1998 (%)	Output index in 1997 (1992=100)			Average annual growth rate of output in 1992-1997 (%)		
		Total	Barter	Non-barter	Total	Barter	Non-barter
Energy	62	81	508	61	− 4	+ 38	− 9
Fuel	48	78	682	50	− 5	+ 47	− 13
Metals	57	79	588	56	− 5	+ 43	− 11
Machinery	58	52	424	31	− 12	+ 33	− 21
Chemicals and petrochemicals	47	62	247	36	− 9	+ 20	− 18
Lumber, pulp and paper	54	47	390	26	− 14	+ 31	− 24
Construction materials	66	45	331	19	− 15	+ 27	− 28
Light industry	47	22	211	12	− 26	+ 16	− 35
Food industry	32	66	385	51	− 8	+ 31	− 13

Sources: Calculated from Goskomstat data and REB Survey statistics

producers of consumer goods is quite approximate as engineering, for example, supplies both types of products, this division is useful to formulate what I believe to be one of the major "laws" of barter trade: *the greater the distance between an industry and final consumption, the larger the share of barter goods in its output.*

The rational for this "law" is quite obvious: producers of consumer goods are limited in their ability to perform exchange in kind since consumers make their purchases for money rather than for other goods. Moreover, consumers use mostly cash because payments in installments or the use credit and debit cards is still very rare in the Russian consumer market. Consequently, if among non-barter goods we group together those sold and bought for cash (C), it becomes evident that the share of consumer goods in this "goods for cash" group is high. Indeed, if we move from barter goods to non-barter goods and further to goods sold for hard cash, the share of consumer goods industries in each category will grow in a rapid progression from 9% to 19% and finally 28% (see Table 3).

TABLE 3. Output by Industry (%)

	Total output (at current prices)		Barter output	Non-barter output, 1997	
	1990	1997	1997	Total	Sold for cash [2]
1. Energy	4.0	17.9	20	16	14
2. Fuel	7.6	18.2	15	21	15
3. Metals	11.5	14.0	19	10	11
4. Machinery	31.5	19.3	19	20	14
5. Chemicals and petrochemicals	7.8	7.6	8	7	8
6. Lumber, pulp and paper	5.8	3.9	4	4	5
7. Construction materials	3.8	4.3	6	3	5
8. Light industries	12.3	1.9	2	2	2
9. Food industry	15.7	12.9	7	17	26
TOTAL [1]	100.0	100.0	100	100	100
Investment goods (1) + (2) + (3) + (4) + (5) + (6) + (7)	72.0	85.2	91	81	72
Consumer goods (8) + (9)	28.0	14.8	9	19	28

[1] Not including other industries and shadow production.
[2] For reference: in 1997 the share of sales for cash in total output was 15%.
Sources: Russian Statistical Yearbook, 1996, 1997, and REB Survey statistics.

The proportion between investment and consumer goods in the goods sold for cash was 72 to 28 in 1997. It is intriguing to note that practically the same ratio between investment and consumer goods was observed in respect to *total* industrial output in 1990, the last year in which the Russian economy showed real growth. Still, it is difficult to say if this is more than a mere coincidence.

THE PROLIFERATION OF BARTER AT THE MICRO-LEVEL

The growth of production for barter in absolute terms was accompanied by the expansion of the range of firms that started to use barter as a selling technique. This latter phenomenon deserves attention. It is possible to state with confidence that though the current extent of barter economy is unique, most Russian industrialists have been familiar with the culture of barter for a long time. According to Makarov and Kleiner (1999), in 1960-80 barter transactions already accounted for 2-6% of total industrial output and their scope continued to expand throughout the final stages of the Soviet period. Experts agree that barter transactions were already quite widely spread prior to price liberalization in 1992. REB statistics give an indirect confirmation to this fact. According to the data in Table 1, in the first year of reforms the average share of barter was relatively small at just 6%. But the degree of the proliferation of barter was already quite remarkable: 59% of REB respondent enterprises were already using barter to some extent. Later, the share of enterprises practicing barter grew further and reached 94% in 1998 (see Table 4). What is more important though is the fact that the first and crucial steps towards the introduction of the "technologies of bartering" were already taken before and not after the start of market reforms.

TABLE 4. Diffusion of Barter and the "Great Barter" in 1992-1998

	Share of enterprises using barter (%)	Share of enterprises with barter reaching over a half of sales (%)
1992	59	0
1993	70	2
1994	79	10
1995	85	17
1996	92	42
1997	93	49
1998	94	55

Source: REB Surveys

The exact timing of the first experience with barter is important for the analysis of the transaction cost of barter. The current transaction cost does not include apparently such a component as the cost of crossing a psychological or cultural threshold of traditional established business behavior. Most Russian industrialists had crossed this threshold long before 1992. As transition started they faced a challenge how to use more thoroughly one of previously known *old patterns* of business activity rather than to introduce a *new* one as an innovative response to environmental changes.

Conceptually the issue of the diffusion of barter transactions may be seen in a somewhat different light. It is possible to assume that barter transactions may be seen as a kind of new organizational "technologies" only after their volume passes a certain critical value, say, 50% of all output of a firm. In this case, we can say with confidence that it was the reform that gave momentum to diffusion of the "great barter." Under this assumption the diffusion of barter may be adequately described with a classical S-shape curve with its typical phases, a turning point in 1995 and saturation after 1996 (see Figure 1).

This interpretation has a considerable potential. While barter transactions were widespread, to push them further beyond a certain critical limit was indeed a big challenge that not many managers were able to cope with considering their psychology and the state of organization of their firms. Where exactly this critical limit laid is a question that for the time being can be answered only tentatively. Indirect information on this limit can be obtained from the data on the distribution of firms by the share of barter turnover (Table 5).

In 1998, as seen from the above data, this distribution had a U-shape form whereof the smallest number of enterprises had the level of barter within the range of 30-50% of sales. To explain this minimum, the following hypothesis may be proposed: there are two states of equilibrium for every firm. One is achieved either at zero or at a negligible level of barter while the other, by contrast, is achieved at the point of very high reliance on barter. Consequently, intermediate states are somewhat ineffective and unstable.

There is no doubt that the parameters of the U-shape distribution have never been constant. The position of the minimum point shifted to the right in the course of general expansion of barter economy. In comparison to previous years, 1998 was marked with the highest level of barterization.

TENTATIVE CONCLUSIONS

Barterization causes a great deal of abnormalities, but it has produced at least one positive result: it helped many experts to dispose of their illusions. In particular, this is relevant to a widespread belief that existing economic theo-

FIGURE 1. Barter versus Money Transactions

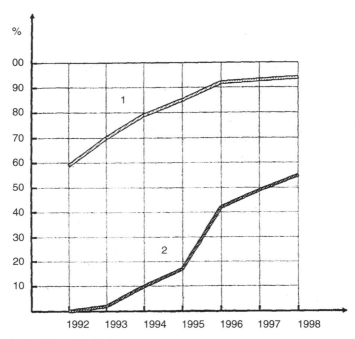

1. Share of enterprises using barter.
2. Share of enterprises in which barter accounts for over half of sales.

ries are generally sufficient for an adequate description of transitional econo-mies. However, the study of the Russian pattern of transition is likely to divert some adepts from this opinion. The failure of reforms in Russia provided con-firmation to the claim of many Russian experts that the economy of their coun-try was specific enough to defy inapt generalization. At the present level of barterization traditional theories of market economy lose their explanatory power. Many facts have to be gathered and analyzed before it would be feasi-ble to put together an adequate theory of transition economy.

Let us consider non-barter goods as an example. They are mostly marketed in a more or less normal way, which means that they are sold for money, either cash or non-cash. There are other non-barter ways of trading such as *increase* in trade receivables. But the share of this latter in total sales is small. There-fore, without risking a serious error, it is possible to state that as far as their non-barter production is concerned Russian manufacturers seek to satisfy *ef-fective demand,* and in this respect they behave quite normally. But then, how

TABLE 5. Distribution of Enterprises by the Share of Barter in Total Sales in 1998 (Average Annual Data)

Share of barter in sales (%)	Share of enterprises (%)
0-10	19
10-20	7
20-30	7
30-40	5
40-50	6
50-60	7
60-70	10
70-80	11
80-90	14
90-100	14

Source: REB surveys.

shall we treat the other part of their output? Barter goods cannot find any effective demand by definition, at least in the conventional sense of this term.

This is one of the points in which the Russian economy has drifted far away from traditional economic theory. In the eyes of many, there is nothing more in this "drift" than damage to efficiency. But such view is too narrow. It is highly likely that if Russian manufacturers had run their businesses "according to the theory" and adjusted their output to effective demand only, crisis in the Russian industry could have been 1.5 times deeper. We could have a 75% rather than the 50% decline in production from the pre-crisis level. Probably the decline could be even steeper, because production costs of barter goods are partly covered with money. Therefore, the elimination of barter output could hurt the effective demand for non-barter goods as well.

It is often alleged that managers of Russian industrial enterprises are guilty of inertia, lack of entrepreneurial spirit, unwillingness to adapt themselves to a new market environment. However, their behavior can be seen in a different light. If, instead of using abstract theoretical criteria, this behavior is evaluated in terms of achievements in relation to the challenges and conditions under which they were forced to operate, firm managers can be praised for wonders of enterprising, a genuine spirit of innovation and a surprisingly independent way of economic thinking as they refused to be intimidated by recommendations given by theoreticians and consultants from all over the world. Indeed, in less than six years they developed from scratch a whole sector of barter economy almost as large as a third of the pre-crisis industry that helped Russia to stay afloat.

It is difficult to overestimate the importance of realizing that barter networks represent a new sector (or sphere) of the economy. On the one hand, it seems to be not quite correct to use the term "sector" in this context, but on the other hand, why not? Indeed, what is barter output? It is the output of *distinctive goods* for sale in *specific markets,* requiring *specific costs and capital outlays* (not just costs of running current barter transactions but also non-recurrent long-term investment in building contacts and relationships that are indispensable for barter networks).

This new sector was supported with capital accumulation within its own boundaries and at the same time, with *capital inflows* from other parts of the economy. Indeed, this inflow was far from conventional. It was bypassing financial markets and allowed avoiding spatial relocation of enterprises and changes of ownership. Nevertheless, it was a flow, and it looked very much similar to inter-industry reallocation of resources. In effect, non-barter output was shrinking and barter output grew like a mushroom.

Finally, assessing pros and cons of barter, we cannot ignore its social value. Actually, it serves as a shock absorber in a crisis environment, allowing enterprises, as well as the government, to win the necessary time for adjustment and further reforms. For this reason, all proposals and calls to "take on the barter" look quite irresponsible. As far as the government is concerned this position can be explained with the concern about tax collection. But what is also quite clear is that under present conditions without barter transactions, much of production in Russia would simply cease to exist rather than be replaced by any form of "normal" or "civilized" production. Theoreticians may argue that it is not dangerous since the general level of value added in Russia could rise, but "practical people" who live in this country may find this sort of argument quite out of touch with the practical needs of the country and its people in the foreseeable future.

REFERENCES

Alchian, A.A. (1977). Why money. *Journal of Money, Credit, and Banking,* 9 (2) 133-140.

Aukutsionek, S. (1998). Barter v rossiyskoi promyshlennosti. *Voprosy ekonomiki,* 2.

Birch, D. and Liesch, P.W. (1998). Moneyless Business Exchange: Practitioner's Attitudes to Business-to-Business Barter in Australia. *Industrial Marketing Management,* 27 (4) July 329-340

Gaddy, C.G. and Ickes, B.I. (1998). Russia's Virtual Economy. *Foreign Affairs,* September/October 53-67.

Makarov, V. and Kleiner,G. (1999). Barter v Rossii: institutsional'nyi etap. *Voprosy ekonomiki,* 4.

Marvasti, A. and Smyth D.J. (1999). The effect of barter on the demand for money: an empirical analysis. *Economics Letters,* 64 (1) July 73-80.

Neale C.W., Shipley, D. and Sercu, P. (1992). Motives for and the Management of Countertrade in Domestic Markets. *Journal of Marketing Management,* 8 335-349.

Williamson, S. and Wright, R. (1994). Barter and monetary exchange under private information. *American Economic Review,* 84 (1) 104-12[3].

SUBMITTED: September 1999
FIRST REVISION: January 2000
SECOND REVISION: March 2000
ACCEPTED: August 2000

Management of Relations
Between Suppliers and Buyers:
The Case of Russia

Julia Popova
Olav Jull Sørensen

ABSTRACT. The aim of this article is to describe and understand the relations between Russian enterprises and their suppliers and buyers as they have developed during the transition years. The overall position of the customers and suppliers is analyzed using the stakeholder theory while the management of the relations is dealt with using three alternative approaches, the mainstream strategic planning approach, the network and the action-experience approach. The findings are based on an empirical study of 172 Russian enterprises. It is found that Russian enterprises do not use strategic planning to any large extent. Financial constraints, the lack of a coherent regulatory framework and imperfect markets make firm managers turn to networking building on experiences from the central planning era. It is also found that networks were instrumental in the fast development of barter trade. However, the networks are weak and unless redefined, are likely to disappear when the financial constraints are overcome. Barter transactions have declined since the financial crisis in August 1998 and following the devaluation of the ruble, producers have experienced new business opportunities, reflected in growing expectations regarding sales and supplies. Given the present

---

[Haworth co-indexing entry note]: "Management of Relations Between Suppliers and Buyers: The Case of RussiaArticle Title." Popova, Julia and Olav Jull Sørensen. Co-published simultaneously in *Journal of East-West Business* (International Business Press, an imprint of The Haworth Press, Inc.) Vol. 6, No. 4, 2001, pp. 37-62; and: *Russian Corporations: The Strategies of Survival and Development* (ed: Andrei Kuznetsov) International Business Press, an imprint of The Haworth Press, Inc., 2001, pp. 37-62.

context, managers are advised to further develop their networks to encompass additional activities, e.g., product and process development, additional domestic customers and suppliers and perhaps additional foreign partners to enhance their technological capabilities. *[Article copies available for a fee from The Haworth Document Delivery Service: 1-800-342-9678. E-mail address: <getinfo@haworthpressinc.com> Website: <http://www. HaworthPress.com> © 2001 by The Haworth Press, Inc. All rights reserved.]*

KEYWORDS. Transition management, network, barter, strategic planning, customer relations, supplier relations

BACKGROUND AND AIM

Although privatization in Russia was by and large implemented in the period from 1992 to 1995 (Boycko, Schleifer and Vishny, 1995), restructuring and reorganization failed to take place within newly privatized firms to any large extent. Furthermore, some developments became prominent that the reformers had not foreseen.

First, the immediate reactions to market reforms on the part of Russian managers was to stick to old suppliers and customers (Svejnar, 1991, Kuznetsov, 1994; Kharkhordin and Gerber, 1994; Boeva and Dolgopyatova, 1994) and to carry on acting in accordance to administrative practices established in the era of central planning.[1] This resulted in enormous arrears in inter-firm payments with no Government to provide support due to the hard credit line introduced as a part of the reforms (Karpov, 1998).

Second, the immediate effect of the reforms was the continuation of the scarcity of supplies (Zawyalov, 1995). Unlike in the years of Soviet planning this scarcity was caused not by the unavailability of goods, but by the lack of working capital to finance the production and transactions. Thus, while production capacity existed, the ability to carry through transactions was restricted.

Third, barter became a predominant form of transactions in goods and services in the Russian economy. The share of barter trade steadily increased from 6% of all transactions in 1992 to a maximum of 51% in 1998, only to decrease to 40-45% in 1999. Financial constraints on firms appear to be the main reason for this phenomenon. It also appears that the stabilization and decline is linked to the August 1998 Government payment crisis when ruble lost three-quarters of its dollar value, causing competition from imports to decline.

Depending on the perspective, these developments are open to different interpretations. From the point of view of the designers of reforms, this is very much synonymous to disaster. It was expected that privatization would kick- start cash-based markets and make transactions transparent. Firm managers did not react as expected and their behavior, notably the accumulation of large arrears, was the closest to ignoring the reforms by creating what amounted to an artificial environment outside normal market conventions. On the other hand, from an organizational point of view, the unparalleled growth of barter trade may be viewed as a remarkable achievement considering (a) the complexity of the task of establishing mutual settlement schemes on such a grand scale; (b) the requirement of being able to handle both cash and barter transactions simultaneously, and (c) the need to closely coordinate the sales/procurement transactions with financial needs. In this context and although at a low level, managers proved to be able to make things work in spite of the reforms.

It is against this background that we set out to study the relations between Russian producers and their customers and suppliers. The aim of the article is to describe how Russian firms manage their relations with customers and suppliers and to explain why they manage the way they do. The conceptual framework for the study will be outlined in the next section, followed by the section on the design of the empirical study and a presentation of the findings. Finally, the theoretical insight and the empirical evidence will be combined and discussed in the concluding section.

CONCEPTUAL FRAMEWORK

Within the marketing literature, relations between producers and buyers have been conventionally studied from the point of view of functional specialization, power, and strategy (Stern and El-Ansary, 1988). More recently, the relationship marketing theory and even more so the network theory have emphasized the importance of long-term co-operative relations between producers, their suppliers and buyers, substituting the arm's length market for the organized market and negotiated environment (Ford, 1997 and 1998). At the same time, the globalization of the economy has formed a platform for extensive research in what has been termed "commodity or value chain management" focusing on the design and management of the totality of the commodity or value chain (Porter, 1985; Gereffi, 1994).

Reviewing the literature (e.g., Holley et al., 1996; Klayner, 1998b), we found that most studies dealing with relations between producers and their suppliers and customers in a transition setting have not been able to explain what is going on in the value chain. Due to the shortage of financial means and efficient financial markets, trade in Russia depends strongly on barter while attempts are made by enterprises to avoid financial mediation involving banks and other financially institutions by introducing so-called "mutual settlement" schemes (Aukutsionek, 1999). These particularities in the interface between Russian enterprises and their suppliers and buyers have forced us to search for supplementary theoretical approaches, expanding the traditional patterns of analysis. We will apply the general Stakeholder Theory in order to investigate the overall role of customers and suppliers within the current set-up in Russia. We will also employ the strategic management approach, the network approach and the action-experience approach in our study. They shall allow us to account for firms with different managerial practices of handling customers and suppliers. For example, it is expected that firms with a great deal of barter trade can be captured by the network approach while the action approach will be helpful in describing firms and situations where it is essential to be on the spot when a business opportunity arises.

The reference point for the our study of relations between customers and suppliers is neither, as in most cases, the norms for optimal market behavior as stipulated in the Western literature (for example, Dicken, 1997) or so-called best practices by Western companies (Paun, 1997), nor the goals and expectations of the reform designers. The reference point is the owners and managers of Russian enterprises themselves, their experience and the environment within which they have to operate and the context they create through their interaction.

The Stakeholder Theory

The stakeholder theory seeks to identify the totality of individuals, groups and organizations that can affect or be affected by the achievements of the organization's objectives (Freeman 1984, p. 46). Thus, the stakeholder theory goes beyond the profit maximization notion of the firm and broadens the tasks and responsibilities of management to include all stakeholders, not just shareholders.

Most studies on stakeholders focus on owners, workers/unions, financial institutions, the government, influential non-market interest groups, etc., while suppliers and buyers attract only marginal interest, despite the fact that the generalized theory of stakeholders unequivocally counts them among stakeholders. The stakeholder theory is based on studies of mature market economies. In a Russian context, the concept of stakeholder is valid but the roles may differ. For example, in addition to being a supplier of goods, a supplier may also be a shareholder and perhaps even be on the board of the buyer. The importance of suppliers and customers as stakeholders will be analyzed using the three attributes developed by Mitchell, Agle and Wood (1997): power, legitimization and urgency. Power means the ability of those who possess power to bring about the outcomes they desire. Power is exercised by coercive, utilitarian, or normative means (p. 865). For example, a buyer may use utilitarian means by taking advantage of his access to cash. Legitimacy includes moral and other claims; i.e., something that is socially desired, accepted and/or expected (p. 866-67). For example, in spite of the reforms, managers were expected to continue to supply their old customers. Urgency indicates that the relations to the stakeholder are important and require the immediate attention of managers (p. 867). For example, the need for cash requires that managers continuously search for customers with access to cash. Although a given relation between two stakeholders, e.g., managers and customers, can be assessed for each of the attributes, the interplay between them is important. Legitimacy, for example, creates authority when combined with power. Without power, " . . . it will not achieve salience for the firm's managers . . . " (Mitchell et al, p. 866).

Strategic Planning Approach

The strategic planning approach is the mainstream approach to strategy formulation and implementation in the mature market economies (de Wit and Meyer, 1994). It has two sub-streams, the outward-in and the inward-out, respectively. The dominant stream is the outward-in in, where it is assumed that the environment (market, competitors, etc.) is the determining factor to which the enterprise has to adapt (Porter 1980). A contesting approach is based on the resource-based theory of the firm, an inward-out approach, where the resources and core competencies of the enterprise are the determining factors of the enterprise strategy (Prahalad and Hamel, 1990; Grant, 1991). As we are focusing on the relations with customers and suppliers, we will primarily use the outward-in approach to strategic planning.

The strategic management approach is also the mainstream approach to marketing. Strategic marketing planning comprises two main activities, i.e., marketing research and the formulation of marketing plans. The strategic marketing plan is formulated on the basis of comprehensive studies of the market demand, the distribution system, and the behavior of customers and competitors. The plan is formulated by top management and in turn, implemented by middle managers

The overall aim of marketing planning is to come to terms with an uncertain environment. The aim of the marketing research is to investigate the uncertainty, and the plan aims to reduce risks to acceptable levels. Thus, strategic planning is difficult, if not impossible, in a very turbulent environment. In this case, managers will have to turn to alternative management instruments to reduce risks, for example, the network approach or the action-experience approach, as presented below.

Most studies of marketing planning investigate the actual extent of market orientation, marketing research and planning activities. For example, Hooley et al. (1996) carried out a comprehensive study of the extent of marketing planning activities in East European enterprises. Richey et al. (1999) investigated the extent of marketing oriented behavior, and Klayner (1998), in his survey of 200 Russian enterprises, used conventional strategic planning as the reference framework. Although many companies, in both mature and transition markets, are found to place relatively little emphasis on planning, the studies rarely provide answers to why they do not plan, what they do instead of planning and what the rationale is for what they are doing. The inclusion in this study of the network and the action approach to customers and suppliers is an attempt to shed some light over these questions.

The Network Concept

The network concept (Ford, 1997; Buttle, 1996) is important for this study because of the role that the networks of managers played in the central planning period and continue to play in modern Russia. Because the managers were not ready to play by the rules set by the designers of the reform program, networks became the basic platform for dealing with the "post-planning" situation. Effectively, the "old" networks formed the foundation for exploring and constructing the Russian version of the market mechanisms.

Within the framework of the network approach, the market is viewed as a set of identifiable and autonomous actors/marketers who, through daily interactions, build long-term relationships with customers and suppliers. These relationships are characterized by trust, allowing to save on transaction costs. Trust also forms a basis for committing resources and mutual development and co-ordination of activities. The network approach implies that focus is on the management of relations rather than on a seller-initiated marketing program (Ford, 1982). That is, the strategy for and the organization of marketing and procurement emerge not so much as the result of stringent and deliberate long-term planning as in the strategic planning approach, but rather in the course of daily interactions within the context of an overall long-term relationship. Planning activities are not ruled out, but they assume mutual alignment between the firm and its long-term customers and suppliers.

The network theory assumes a general atmosphere of co-operation and mutual interest among network participants, rather than opportunism, as in the transaction cost theory. Nonetheless, network participants struggle for position providing them with a better access to resources and information. At the same time, some outsiders will be waiting to enter the network if certain traditional links within the structure get weaker. In addition, networks are normally not stable. They change and grow by attracting new partners with the help of using existing partners. Inside the network, the information flow is relatively open and ideas get developed through the daily interaction between the participants. In this way, information gathered through networks may substitute for formal marketing research and planning. As a result, the market is not "read" and interpreted by the firm through a formal market research but rather it is treated as an extension of one's own organization.

A number of researchers studied relations in Russia using the network theory. Salmi (1996) outlines the principles of what managers must do if they work under network conditions; Lehtinen (1996) focuses on relationship marketing; Popova and Sørensen (1996) use the network theory to investigate and understand the reactions of Russian enterprises to economic reforms. Huber and Wörgötter (1998) divide the whole of the Russian economy into "entrepreneurial networks" and "survival networks," the former comprising the profit-oriented enterprises which have adapted to the new market conditions and the latter struggling to survive within closed and relatively stable networks, the main purpose of which is to extract rents. According to the authors, survival networks pre-dominate Russia. Johanson, Kushesh, and Silver (2000) deviate from most research by stating that networks hardly existed in the pre-reform period. They found from case studies in 1997 that even although enterprises had supply links to each other before the reforms, they had very little knowledge of each other. Furthermore, in spite of the market turmoil, they tended to neglect the role of trust and commitment. Finally, Rose (2000) studied network building based on the concept of social capital, focusing on how informal networks are developed to overcome short-comings in the current Russian economy. The study is part of an interesting project on social capital as a property of cultures, individuals or situations.

The Action-Experience Approach

The action-experience approach to managing a firm entails that the firm relies on its experiences and ability to act rather than on long-term planning. This approach is useful in particular when, as in Russia, the environment is turbulent and access to information about business opportunities is difficult. However, the action-experience approach is also used in less turbulent situations by managers who are good at spotting market opportunities, impatient, intuitive and who possess a strong action capacity. This type of manager can be found in both large but especially in small and medium-sized companies (OECD, 1997). In the latter case, the manager who often is also the owner is both the center of excellence and control and decision making. In the case of a larger firm, the action capacity must be built into "strategic management" which, unlike "strategic planning," is characterized by the following activities and capabilities:

- the continuous monitoring of the environment,
- the drawing of discrete scenarios of the future,
- the building of financial and managerial capacity,
- broad based strategy discussions and formulations,
- the building of implementation and action capacity.

This approach to management is not too well presented in the literature because the action manager is not easy to tie down in a model (Kuada and Sorensen, 1997). This type of manager resembles the entrepreneur as she is assumed in the Austrian School of Economics (Reekie, 1989) with its emphasis on dynamics and disequilibrium caused by entrepreneurial activity. The approach also draws on the practices of Japanese managers who more actively participate in the market to acquire experience upon which they can act (Johansson and Nonaka, 1987).

In Russia, the action manager can be found in many short-term oriented companies displaying opportunistic behavior as observed by de Wit and Monani (1994). However, the action approach to management can also be found in firms which are forced to be more action oriented due to the turbulence in their markets or due to the simple fact that they do not know how to plan and learn from active participation. In this sense, the action-experience approach represents a mode of management that is very natural to adopt when facing new and unknown realities. This potential to adapt by contemporary Russian managers was spotted earlier (Kuznetsova and Kuznetsov, 1996) and is confirmed again by the data we collected in the course of our survey.

Figure 1 provides the overview and comparison of the three approaches to managing customer-supplier relations. The approaches are analytically distinct. However, in practice we expect them to be mixed although different managers may have inclinations towards using one of them. For easy reference, in the following sections the three approaches will be denominated as the Planning Man, the Action Man and the Networker.

EMPIRICAL FINDINGS

The Format of the Survey

The REB-panel of Russian firms[2] was used for this study of suppliers and customers. The survey for this study was carried out in August 1999, a year after a major crisis caused by the default of the Russian Government on its

FIGURE 1. The Planning, the Network and the Action-Experience Approach

Approach:	Planning	Network	Action-Experience
Characteristics of Managers	• Analytical minded • Order • Control	• Social • Trust • Security	• Action • Independence • Impatience • Intuitive
Business Formula	• Plan and implement • Planned growth	• Search and interact • Emerging development	• Spot and act • Leap frogging in its development
Relation to Environment	• Accept and adapt • Collect information	• Relate and create • Build long-term relations	• Create and impose • Search for opportunities

short-term debt. The sample comprised 173 industrial firms. The response rate of 35% was achieved.

At the preparatory stage preceding the survey five interviews were carried out with firms in the Republic of Komi in Russia. The results of the interviews helped to formulate questions in a manner that assured relevant answers. The questionnaire comprised 22 questions split into three main groups dealing with the main characteristics of the firm; the structure of ownership, the style of management, and relationships between customers and suppliers, and the third group comprises a few questions related to the impact of the August 1998 crisis.

Profile of Sample Firms

Firms for the survey were selected to be representative of the current structure of Russian firms. By Russian standards, approximately 67% of the firms in the survey are of medium size, 17% are large and 16% are small. The average number of employees per respondent is 752 and sales turnover was Rbl. 56 millions (US$ 9-10 million) in 1998. In terms of a legal status, the absolute majority of surveyed firms, 94%, are former state-owned firms, of which 85% have been privatized to become joint-stock companies and 14% are still state owned. Only 2% of sample are newly established private entities. Finally, the panel comprises 4% of firms under other forms of ownership.

General Economic Situation

Managers were asked to describe the overall situation of their firms in terms of finance, sales and supply (Table 1). Half of them stated that the financial situation was very bad or bad while 42% said it could be better. Only 8% regarded their financial circumstances as satisfactory and none thought that they

TABLE 1. How Would You Characterize the General Situation and Development of the Firm? (% of Respondents)

		Present situation					Expected changes in the situation		
		Very good	Good	Satisfactory	Not Good	Bad	Improving	Remains the same	Deteriorating
A	Financial situation	0	8	42	38	12	26	61	13
B	Sales	0	19	55	24	2	35	54	11
C	Supply	1	12	49	33	5	14	71	15

were very good. Encouragingly, only 13% claimed the financial situation to have been deteriorating while 61% expected it to remain the same and 26% anticipated improvements.

In terms of sales, 26% of respondents stated that the situation was very bad or bad while 55% said it could be better. Almost a fifth of firms had satisfactory sales, but none very good. Talking about expectations, managers were more optimistic in their evaluation of sales perspectives in comparison with the financial developments. More than one third (35%) expect improvement, while 54% expect sales to remain at the same level. Only 11% predicted sales to decrease.

The state of supplies appears to be somewhat worse than that of sales: 38% of received responses characterized it as very bad or bad; 49% said it could be better. By contrast, only 12% of respondents believed that their supply situation is satisfactory and just 1% judged it to be very good. As regards the future, most managers (71%) expected the supply situation to remain the same with an equal split of the remaining answers between those who expected deterioration and those anticipating an improvement.

Thus, overall the situation is not good. To sustain all three major parameters (finance, sales and procurement) at a minimally satisfactory level, the management is routinely required to put in efforts considerably exceeding what would be reasonable under normal market conditions. However, on a positive side, relatively few managers (10-15%) expect further deterioration of the business environment.

Changes in Ownership Structure

The ownership structure of the individual firm was measured ordinally on a 5-point scale. The managers were asked to assign 1 to the group of owners with the largest batch of shares, 2 for the next largest and so on. Workers emerged as the main owner group with the average of 1.85 points, followed by the state (2.10), other firms (2.23), managers (2.37) and other individuals (2.94). This ownership profile is in accordance with the findings of other studies, and appears to reveal a solid grip that employees (workers and managers) have on the firms.

The managers were asked about any significant changes in the ownership structure since 1995. In 76% cases, there had been no such changes. Asked about the present stability in the ownership structure, little more than a third (36%) found it to be stable and 51% characterized it as relatively stable while 14% awaited changes due to an unsettled situation.

As this study is concerned with the relations between customers and suppliers, the managers were also asked about the ownership position of these groups. It was found that 18% of long-term customers and 9% of long-term suppliers possessed shares in the sample firms. The managers were also asked if those customers and suppliers who own shares hold a board position. According to responses, 21% of buyers-shareholders and 18% of suppliers-shareholders held such positions. Interestingly, some firms reported that they had board members representing suppliers and buyers who were not shareholders.

The sample data show that buyers are twice as likely to own shares of the firms-respondents as suppliers are. This may indicate that, despite efforts by the government to liberalize the markets and encourage competition, suppliers have an advantage over buyers very much like in the period of central planning. It may also point at the precarious financial position of buyers who may have offered shares in a settlement of payment arrears. At the same time only 5% of the responding managers reported that their firm held shares of their customers or suppliers. This is considerably lower than the share of customers and suppliers who keep shares of the firms-respondents.

Investments in Subsidiaries

The managers gave the following answers to the question about the establishment of subsidiaries and links with them: 86% of firms had no subsidiaries; 7% had one; 4% two; 2% had three, and 1% three or more. Firms establish subsidiaries mostly to facilitate sales although the desire to secure supplies emerged as the second in importance objective. Subsidiaries providing services, e.g., canteens hold the third place. Finally, a few firms have established subsidiaries with no functional linkage to the respondent's firm.

Product Portfolio and Competing Products

The respondents were asked to provide information on three major products in their assortment. Table 2 provides the summary of the data. On average, the firms turned out to be relatively specialized with the main product accounting

TABLE 2. Product Portfolio of the Firms

	Product 1	Product 2	Product 3
% of sales of the three main products	59	24	17
Standard (S) or differentiated product (D)	S: 83 D:17	S: 83 D: 17	S: 76 D: 24
No. of competing products presently in the market: None 1-3 4 or more:	0-5% 1-3– 37% 4.... 58%	0-7% 1-3–32% 4.... 61%	0-10% 1-3–30% 4.... 59%
No. of customers: One-two, 3-10, or 11 or more	1-2– 8% 3-10–13% 11.... 79%	1-2–7% 3-10- 26% 11....67%	1-2- 9% 3-10–25% 11.... 66%
Type of product: Industrial (I) or consumer (C) or both (B):	I-40% C-39% B-21%	I-63% C-26% B-12%	I-59% C-26% B-15%
Is the product exported (directly by your firm or indirectly by others)	Y- 32% N- 68%	Y-24% N- 76%	Y- 21% N- 79%

for 59% of sales. The second and third most important products account for 24% and 17%, respectively. It should be noticed that these figures are not based on total sales, but calculated on the basis of sales for the three main products.

By type, the main output in 40% of firms are industrial goods and in 39% of firms–consumer products. The remaining 21% of respondents sell both on industrial and consumer markets. In case of product no. 2 and 3, industrial products dominate (63% and 59%, respectively) while consumer products account for 26% in both cases.

The managers characterize their products as standard, i.e., as carrying no distinctive qualities differentiating it from other similar products in the market, in 83%, 83%, and 76% of cases, respectively, for the three main products, the rest being differentiated products. Even if these are very high figures and that there may be some uncertainty as to how the managers have defined the concepts of standard/differentiated product, there is no doubt that the firms are not practicing product differentiation to any large extent.

To assess the intensity of competition, the managers were asked about the number of competing products. Contrary to what is claimed sometimes in the literature about the degree of competition in the Russian market, only 5% of respondents thought that they had a position close to monopoly for their main product. Almost 60% of producers asserted that there were 4 or more competing products. For product no. 2 and 3, the situation is similar, except that 10% of the firms maintained that they have a monopoly situation in case of product 3. Asked more directly, 12% of the managers answered positively to the question "Do you think that your firm is a monopolist on the market?" At the same time 71% said "no" and 17% replied "it is difficult to say." When asked to qualify the degree of competition, 30% said that competition was very sharp or sharp and 18% found the competition to be weak or very weak, i.e., half of the firms rated competition as "not sharp and not weak."

Finally, the managers were asked about export. The main product was exported directly or indirectly by one third of the firms. For the 2nd and 3rd ranking product, the export share was 24% and 21%, respectively.

Overall, the simultaneous existence of standard products and a number of competing suppliers imply that, in principle, buyers should have access to alternative sources of supply without incurring prohibitive transaction and switching costs. However, it should also be noted that only 30% of the managers found themselves to be in a very competitive situation. This indicates that although alternative sources of supplies exist, they are not necessarily readily available. As will be shown later, other factors may prevent the customers from choosing freely among suppliers.

Sources of Supplies

The managers were questioned about three main supplies. Again, it was found that most of them consist of standard products (83%, 87% and 83%). Furthermore, most firms rely on domestic supplies (see Table 3). Over 80% of the respondent firms never use import as a source for main supplies. Only between 2 to 4% of the enterprises imported all of the three main inputs. Overall, 12-18% of the respondents claimed that they had no alternative suppliers of the three main inputs, while 40%, 43% and 54% had 1-3 and 45%, 39% and 37% had 4 or more alternative suppliers of the three main inputs, respectively. Two thirds of the respondents maintained that it would be difficult to replace the present supplier of the three main inputs. This finding is supported by the data on the share of supplies delivered by the key providers.

The difficulty of replacing a supplier is further stressed by the discovery that the change of supplier occurs only very rarely: on average, the duration of a relationship with the main supplier has been 14, 12 and 11 years, respectively, for the three key supplies.

TABLE 3. Main Suppliers and the General Supply Situation

	Product 1	Product 2	Product 3
Is the supply item imported: Totally (T); To some extent (E); Not at all (N)	T-2% E-14% N-84%	T-3% E-12% N-85%	T-4% E-13% N-83%
Is the supply a standard (S) or differentiated product (D)	S-83% D-17%	S-87% D-13%	S-83% D-17%
No. of competing suppliers from whom you easily can get supplies: None (N), Few 1-3 (F), Many 4 and more (M)	N-15% F-40% M-45%	N-18% F-43% M-39%	N-12% F-54% M-37%
Is the supplier difficult (D) or easy (E) to replace	D-68% E-32%	D-72% E-28%	D-64% E-36%
Duration of relationship with main supplier (years)	14	12	11

Relations with Customers

Apart from questions related to products and competition, the managers were asked about the way they interacted with customers. The survey revealed that only 51% of the firms had a marketing department. Cash sales accounted for 48% in 1997 and 1998 and increased to 55% in 1999. This finding is in accordance with the Russian Economic Barometer's survey (Aukutsionek, 1999), and it should be noted that the change in the trend seems to coincide with the payment crisis in August 1998. As regards the number of customers, respondents had 11 or more in 79%, 67% and 66% cases for the three main products. However, up to 9% of the firms had just one to two customers.

Almost 35% of the respondents reported that buyers from before the start of economic reforms were responsible for the largest share of sales. For 48% of firms, customers acquired in the period between 1992 and 1997 were the most important and 15% of respondents pointed at new customers acquired in 1998 or later as providing the highest share of sales. Thus, with two thirds of the buyers acquired after the reforms started, the claim that the customer base of Russian firms depends on "old chaps" is not valid anymore.

To get a feel for the power relations between the firm and its customers, managers were asked to provide answers on a 5-point scale to a set of statements (see Table 4). The firms reported that in 49% of cases, they determine the conditions of sales. At the same time, the majority of firms (74%) rate themselves very highly regarding the issue of flexibility and willingness to listen and adjust to customer requests. Almost 40% of respondents claim that sales contracts are

TABLE 4. How Would You Characterize Your Relations to Your Main Customers ("5"-Completely Agree, "1"-Completely Disagree)

		5	4	3	2	1
A	Customers determine primarily the conditions of sales	15%	17%	35%	19%	14%
B	We determine primarily the conditions of sales	18%	31%	34%	9%	8%
C	We are flexible and willing to listen and adjust to customer requests	43%	31%	21%	5%	0%
D	Sales contracts are concluded after much negotiation	18%	18%	37%	18%	9%
E	We have a long-term standard agreement with our main customers. It is more or less automatically renewed each year	19%	22%	25%	15%	20%

concluded after much negotiations, while 41% maintain that they have a standard agreement which is more or less automatically agreed upon each year.

Relations to Suppliers

Almost two third of the managers agree with the statement that suppliers in the main determine the conditions of buying (see Table 5). Furthermore, suppliers are not found to be very flexible and listen to the requests from the firm. One third of respondents agree strongly or relatively strongly to the statement that procurement contracts are concluded after much negotiation and almost half disagree with the statement that a standard contract is more or less automatically renewed every year.

Combining the findings presented in Tables 4 and 5, we may conclude that suppliers are in a dominant position and have the upper hand in the negotiations of contracts. This ties in with the statement by respondents that their firms find it difficult to replace main suppliers and that the duration of the relations with suppliers are of long-term nature–more than 10 years, on the average.

Finally, it is probably telling about the human nature that respondent managers, while agreeing that suppliers dominate, prefer to believe that when they are in the position of supplier, they show more flexibility towards their clients than their own suppliers are ready to show towards them.

The Consequences of the 1998 Crisis

Since the default in the payment of debts of the Russian government in August 1998, 55% of the respondent firms have experienced a growth of sales and

TABLE 5. How Would You Characterize Your Relations to Your Main Suppliers ("5"-Completely Agree, "1"-Completely Disagree)

F	The suppliers determine in the main the conditions of buying	32%	30%	22%	9%	7%
G	We determine in the main the conditions of buying	9%	12%	27%	30%	22%
I	The suppliers are flexible and listen and adjust to our requests	9%	13%	30%	31%	17%
H	Procurement contracts are concluded after much negotiation	18%	16%	34%	22%	10%
J	We have a long-term standard agreement with our suppliers which is more or less automatically renewed each year	13%	18%	24%	24%	22%

only 18% faced a decline. Similarly, 22% of the firms have increased employment while 25% have released some labor. In the majority (53%) of firms, the employment has not changed.

The managers were also asked about the impact of the 1998 crisis in case their firms used imported supplies. Table 6 shows that in 50% of cases, the influence was modest, as the firms relied on imports only marginally. One third of the respondents agreed and 41% disagreed with the statement that it was relatively easy to find a Russian supplier to substitute for a foreign supplier. In the opinion of the managers, Russian suppliers took advantage of the situation and increased their prices while only a minority chose to increase production. Almost 40% of the managers supported the statement that Russian substitutes could be found but that the quality of their produce was not good enough. Overall, 64% of firms believed they were very much affected by a shift from foreign to local suppliers, while 24% stated that they were not affected at all.

Management Style

Building upon the concepts of the Planning Man, Action Man and the Networker explained earlier, six statements were offered for evaluation to our respondents (see Table 7). Two thirds of the managers agreed both to the statement that (1) intuition and experience are more important than formal marketing analysis and (2) good customer relations are more important than formal marketing research. Furthermore, 59% of the managers supported the statement that (3) in a turbulent market, it is more important to react to market signals than to plan market activities. Along the same line, 50% stated that (4) market turbulence makes planning difficult. Finally, 50% claimed that they act immediately when an opportunity arises and do not await any detailed analysis of the

TABLE 6. If You Use Imported Supplies, How Did the August 1998 Crises Influence Your Supply Situation ("5"- Completely Agree, "1"-Completely Disagree):

	Statement	5	4	3	2	1
A	Not very much as we use very little imported supplies	44	6	10	13	28
B	It was relatively easy to find Russian suppliers	20	14	25	13	28
C	Russian suppliers took advantage of the situation and increased their prices	58	19	8	2	12
D	Russian suppliers have reacted promptly and increased production	8	15	28	26	22
E	We found new Russian supplier but the quality was not good enough	26	12	22	15	24
F	We use a lot of imported supplies but crises didn't influence our supply situation	14	10	12	22	42

TABLE 7. Management Style of Russian Managers

	Statement	5	4	3	2	1
A	Intuition and market experience is more important than market reports and formal planning of sales activities	36	30	22	6	5
B	When a market opportunity arises, we act immediately and do not analyze the opportunity in detail	21	29	32	13	5
D	We use formal marketing analysis primarily to confirm our own ideas	22	18	29	18	12
C	Good customer relations are more important than formal marketing plans and strategy	35	31	21	8	5
E	In a turbulent market it is more important to be able to react to market signals than to plan market activities	31	28	24	9	8
F	Market turbulence makes planning difficult	35	21	18	12	14

new opportunity (5). This indicates that Russian managers act more like Networkers and Action Men, i.e., for them active and daily market participation is more important than planning.

DISCUSSION

The present Russian economic context is rather fluid. This increases the difficulty of interpreting the data. Russian managers together with other influential stakeholders are in the midst of creating what eventually will become the

Russian version of the market economy and our survey has shown that, compared to mature market economies, the interface between Russian enterprises and their buyers and suppliers is managed differently. A set of peculiarities have been identified, although it is yet to be seen to what extent they will become permanent features of the emerging market economy in Russia. The findings give rise to a number of theoretical implications.

Customers and Suppliers as Stakeholders

The strength of the stakeholder approach is that it invites one to study all aspects of relations between the enterprise and stakeholders. In addition to the transactional relations between firms and their customers and suppliers, we have included in this study ownership relations, i.e., the extent of cross-ownership between producers, suppliers and buyers. As indicated earlier, the importance of a stakeholder group can be measured by the urgency with which their interests are attended to, the legitimate claims they have on the firm, and the power relations between the group and the firm. This study cannot provide detailed data on all three issues, but it is still possible to get an impression of the positions of the suppliers and buyers in the value chain.

As to *urgency,* the speed with which barter trade was adopted indicates how important the relations with customers and suppliers are. At the same time, the need for cash to pay salaries, taxes, bills for services, etc., forced the enterprises to seek customers with access to cash. For example, in one case enterprise, the salesmen were assessed on the amount of cash they could bring home from customers. Therefore, buyers paying cash are likely to have a firmer grip on their suppliers.

The issue of *legitimate claims* is a difficult one in the present Russian situation. The main problem is to choose the terms of reference for evaluating the righteousness—legal or ethical—of a claim. For example, when the reforms were started in 1992, industrial firms continued to supply their old customers, even if they could not pay, leading to a build-up of arrears (Gurkov, 1998). This could be labeled bad management, but it could also be seen as a legitimate claim embedded in traditional practices and well-established networks. Furthermore, due to the cash constraints, managers have formed closed networks to avoid taxes by using barter trade, or to extract resources from the Government (Huber and Wörgötter 1998). This can be seen as an example of unethical behavior, but there is no doubt this was also an important part of the survival strategy of the firms, and thus a legitimate act to protect other stakeholders. Thus, it depends on the point of reference whether these and other transaction-related practices are interpreted as legitimate or illegitimate. Puffer (1999) has found that the ethics of Russian managers on several points are different from the ethics of American managers. Apart from cultural differences, this can be explained with reference to past experiences and the present context. With only a tentative regulatory framework in place (Lucas and Maltsev, 1996; Kuznetsova and Kuznetsov, 1996) and too little time for the stakeholder groups to have established their own checks and monitoring procedures, only personal morals and claims on each other put restrictions on business practices. To deal with the present situation, managers have created networks. The networks have made it possible to continue to do business. They have also included members who can assist in overcoming the deficiencies in the regulatory framework. Furthermore, by developing rules internal to the network partners, networks are able to restrict opportunism to unfold. In other words, networks are instrumental in creating a legitimacy of its own.

The legitimacy of networks in Russia has been under much attack, being described as harmful to the Russian economy partly due to the use of "sticky" old practices (Huber and Wörgötter, 1998). Indeed, there is little doubt that networks are used for rent-seeking purposes. Nonetheless, role of networks must not be underestimated. The ability of Russian managers to network has also been instrumental in introducing barter transactions in the cash-deprived Russian economy. Without this capability based on pre-reform experiences, the economic situation in Russia would have been much worse than it is today. Furthermore, although long-term relations exist, our survey shows that only 33% of the customers date back to the pre-reform period.

As regards the issue of *power,* the empirical findings indicate that suppliers have a stronger position than customers (Table 4 and 5). The survey also shows that producers only to a limited extent establish subsidiaries with the aim of strengthening their sales and supply base. Furthermore, as shown earlier, relatively few customers and suppliers hold shares in the enterprise of the respondent and visa-versa. These findings suggest that no big power game take place between enterprises and their customers and suppliers. However, our earlier case studies have indicated that Russian firms make attempts to strengthen their control over sales and avoid middlemen. For example, firms extend their sales organization in order to be closer to customers and thus take advantage of the actual demand whenever it arises (Popova and Sorensen, 1997). Furthermore, firms have increasingly established "commercial departments" to manage barter transactions (Gurkov, 1998, p. 269). Finally, surveys have shown that managers establish and own firms that control the supplies to and sales from the very enterprise they manage (Gurkov and Asselberg, 1995; Bim, 1996).

In general, when designing the present study, our expectations were that customers and suppliers as stakeholders were very important and that we would be able to identify clear power structures and claims on the enterprise. This has not been the case. There may be a simple explanation of the discrepancy between our expectations and the results of the survey. Although buyers and sellers in principle have opposite interests, it may well be that, in accordance with the network theory, relations between them are built more on the principles of mutuality than coercion. Barter deals require reciprocity and understanding. Our findings that 60% of the managers contend that good customer relations are more important than formal marketing strategy and planning and that the firms normally have long-term relations (above 10 years) with their suppliers indicate this. Such response came even from firms that dealt mainly in standard products under competitive conditions and had allegedly easy access to alternative sources of supplies. Obviously, financial constraints imposed by the reforms put these alternative sources out of reach. To overcome this barrier, managers are forced to use partly their networks from the planning era, partly their ability to create new networks and thus put together transaction mechanisms like barter and mutual settlement schemes.

Planning Man, Action Man or Networker

The results of our survey have clearly shown that Russian managers are not involved in strategic planning to any large extent. They use a more participative mode of management, i.e., they have inclinations similar to the Action Man and the Networker in their dealings with the suppliers and customers. Several factors may be held accountable for this.

For obvious reasons, strategic planning techniques were not part of the management toolbox during the central planning period. More importantly, the current turmoil in the Russian market makes long-term and even medium-term planning worthless. The style of participative management is more appropriate under these circumstances. Furthermore, as indicated in Table 1, financial constraints make managers turn to networks. The latter may be either simple dyadic relations around barter deals or elaborate structures reaching almost from one end of the value chain to the other. Reliance on networks does not mean that managers may neglect constantly looking for opportunities outside the networks. Considering the sporadic nature of the Russian market, it is paramount for the manager to be alert and in accordance with the action-experience approach to management to have the capacity to act swiftly when a potential demand is spotted.

Our findings on the use of strategic management seem to be in contradiction with the recent study by Klayner (1998). He investigated 200 Russian enterprises and found that 68% had some experiences in strategic planning of which two thirds found the experience to be positive. Furthermore, 60% of those with the positive experience had a normal financial situation. Enterprises with no experience in strategic planning found that the environment was too turbulent for strategic plans to be made or their immediate survival had top priority. Enterprises with some experience indicated the following difficulties with implementing strategic planning: 25% lacked recommendations and good study materials; 23% mentioned the lack of experience; another 23% were in doubt of the need for strategic plans and 20% claimed that they were overwhelmed by routine work and thus found it difficult to find the time for planning. It is interesting to note that, when asked about what they considered as strategic decisions, the managers did not regard as such the recruiting of staff and business partners, or the emission of shares.

A closer comparison between the findings by Klayner and our own show that they are not as contradictory as it may appear. First of all, the questionnaire used by Klayner forced respondents into a specific way of thinking because it only asked them about the degree of strategic planning and did not mention, as in our study, other modes of management. Secondly, for some unexplained reasons, many of enterprises in Klayner's sample have a normal financial situation. We would also have expected more interest in strategic planning from our respondents had they not faced a survival situation on a daily basis. Finally, the analysis of Klayner's data allows one to assume that for the Russian managers of the survey, the term "strategic planning" had a different meaning compared to what is accepted in the West.

To conclude, progress in managerial competence in the handling of customers and suppliers cannot be measured by the degree to which Russian managers practice strategic planning the Western way. The Russian context is different and more complex and the Russian mindset is different too (Holden, 2000; Puffer, 1999). In the present context, managers use a more participative mode of management with strategies emerging through actual market inter-action rather than being deliberately planned (Håkansson and Snehota, 1990).

Barter versus Cash Transactions

In the present situation, Russian firms have to establish and manage two transaction mechanisms, barter and cash. Surveys indicate that, on the average, the two mechanisms provide an equal share of all transactions. However, looking at individual enterprises, Aukutsionek (1999) found that firms tend to have either a very small share of barter in their turnover or a very large share of 70% and above. The middle position is avoided and the choice depends very much on the industry. This attitude is quite understandable, having in mind that transaction costs will increase if the enterprise operates both systems simultaneously.

As indicated above, the growth of barter trade may be related to the ability to network, negotiate and operate without much financial management that managers carried with them from the planning era. However, barter networks are not stable. They exist to address a very specific problem, the shortage of cash. If the shortage is overcome, the role of networks will decrease. This is related to the nature of cash as a generic resource. Networks based on cash generate no tacit knowledge unique to the partners in the network. Consequently, networks, at least in the form they exist in Russia, will lose their unique advantage if cash transactions replace barter transactions, with an improvement in the financial situation of the enterprises. This does not mean, of course, that networks will disappear altogether. More complex and durable networks may emerge based on more differentiated resources. For example, in one of the case enterprises, an affiliate was established close to a main customer in order to be able to build long-term and strong relations with the customer in the area of product development, product adaptation, etc. However, this type of networking is still rare in Russia.

The Implications of the August 1998 Crisis

The data from this survey were collected approximately one year after the economic crisis in August 1998, and they show that managers in general are a little more optimistic as to the future than previously (Table 1). At the same time, barter trade in Russia stopped growing and even declined in 1999. One reason for this could be that when imports and especially the imports of consumer goods came to an almost standstill as a result of the crisis, this freed some cash flows for the domestic circulation of goods. A second reason could be that export increased and the price of oil went up, pouring more money into Russia. This indicates that barter is very sensitive to the availability of cash and working capital.

Furthermore, the crisis gave those Russian firms that did not depend on imports some breathing space. The devaluation of the rouble made Russian products more competitive on the international markets while local producers could re-establish themselves or expand as the imports of finished goods had been all but wiped out. For example, in one of our cases, the producer of non-woven materials started supplying materials, to a Russian producer of plastic-coated tablecloths again after a long break. As a matter of fact, the importers/traders of foreign finished goods were forced to turn to home producers in order to be able to satisfy the customer network, which they have established as importers.

CONCLUSIONS AND RESEARCH IMPLICATIONS

Relations between firms and their customers and suppliers cannot be understood without giving due attention to the Russian context, with its imperfect markets and incoherent regulatory system, and to the mindset of managers as developed during the planning era and the first years of the economic reforms. Studies using the formulas borrowed from Western textbook or best practices will not be able to explain what goes on in Russia, let alone come up with proper guidelines. Furthermore, Russian managers do not operate in accordance with a single and simple formula, and it is thus wrong to make hard categorizations of Russian firms, such as "survival networks" and "entrepreneurial networks" (Huber and Wörgötter, 1998) or market-oriented versus non-market-oriented managers (Richey et al., 1999). Russian managers use mostly participatory management (networking and action orientation) with strategies emerging from the experiences gained through market operations rather than planned deliberately. In their relations with customers and suppliers, normal market transactions are mixed with networking where economic activities are socially embedded. The networks created have the additional purpose of creating an operational space to overcome the deficiencies of the regulatory framework and the market turbulence. Any research design has to reflect these facts and, when measuring managerial orientation, provide alternative management modes to choose from. The implications for management are that as long as cash constraints prevail, managers should continue to strengthen their networks. However, they should also embark on using the networks for other purposes than barter transactions, including the improvements of products and production processes in close co-operation with customers and suppliers. Furthermore, they should use their present network position to include new domestic partners and explore the possibilities for including foreign partners who may want to establish joint ventures or strategic alliances, and thus get access to the Russian market or sources of supplies.

Overall, it is important to realize that a market economy does not develop according to a simplistic formula. Russia has and will develop its own particularities based on its historical roots and formed by the experiences and present practices of the Russian investors and managers. One of these particularities will not, as shown in this study, be barter trade. Russia will have a full-fledged cash economy. Networks will be important, but for other purposes and reasons.

NOTES

1. Some of these management practices are: Supply, technical and command orientation; negotiation skills; personal network building and alliances with workers; arranging and manipulating data rather than analyzing them for problem solving purposes; skeptical of improvements as they may endanger fulfilling the production target. This profile clearly shows that Russian managers do not use strategic planning but the more participative management modes, using the powerful position of the manager to act in the market.

2. Since December 1991, the "Russian Economic Barometer" (REB) has conducted panel surveys of Russian firm managers. The sample comprises about 500 industrial firms. The response rate varies from 30-40%. Industrial firms, selected for the sample, are situated rather evenly over the territory of Russia and all branches of industry are represented.

REFERENCES

Aukutsionek, S. (1999). Barter: New data and Comments. Russian Economic Barometer. (3) 3-16.

Aukutsionek, S. (1998). Industrial Barter in Russia. *Communist Economics & Economic Transformation,* 10 (2) 179-188.

Bim. A. S. (1996). Ownership, Control over the Enterprise, and Strategies of the Stockholders. IILSA Working paper, WP 96-050. Laxenburg, Austria: International Institute for Applied Systems Analysis (IILSA).

Boeva, I. and Dolgopyatova, T. (1994). State Enterprises during Transition: Forming Strategies for Survival. In A. Aaslund (ed.), Economic Transformation in Russia. London: Pinter, pp. 111-127.

Boycko, M., Shleifer, A. and Vishny, R.(1995). *Privatizing Russia.* Cambridge, Mass.: MIT-Press.

Buttle, F. (ed.) (1996). *Relationship Marketing: Theory and Practice.* London: Paul Chapman Publishing Co.

De Wit, A. and Monami, E. (1994): Understanding the Former Soviet Market: An Interaction Approach. In Buckley, P. J. and P. N. Ghauri (eds) The Economics of Change in East and Central Europe. London: Academic Press, 279-296.

De Wit, B. and Meyer, R. (Eds) (1994). *Strategy. Process, Content, Context.* New York: West Publishing Company.

Dicken, Peter R. (1997). *Marketing Management,* 2nd ed. New York: The Dryden Press.

Dolgopiatova, T. and Euseyeva, I. (1995). Economic Behavior of the Industrial Enterprises in the Transition Economy. Communist Economies and Economic Transformation 7 (3) 319-31.

Earle, J. S., Estrin, S. and Leshchenko, L. (1996). Ownership Structures, Patterns of Control, and Firm Behavior in Russia. In Cammander, S., Fun, Q. and Schaffer, M. (eds) *Firm Restructuring and Economic Policy in Russia.* Washington D.C.: World Bank: 205-251

Ford, D. (1980). Development of Buyer-Seller Relationships in Industrial Markets. *European Journal of Marketing,* 14 (5/6) 339-354.

Ford, D. (1997). *Understanding Business Markets: Interaction, Relationship and Networks.* 2nd ed. London: Dryden Press.

Ford, D. et. al (1998). *Managing Business Relations.* New York: John Wiley & Sons.

Freeman, R.E. (1994). The Politics of Stakeholder Theory: Some Future Directions. *Business Ethics Quarterly,* 4 (4), 409-421.

Freeman, R.E. (1984). *Strategic Management: A Stakeholder Approach.* Boston: Pitman.

Gereffi, G. (1994). The Organization of Buyer-Driven Global Commodity Chains: How U.S. Retailers Shape Overseas Production Networks. In G. Gereffi and M.

Korzeniewicz (eds.), Commodity Chains and Global Capitalism. Praeger: London, 95-122.

Grant, R. (1991). The Resource Based Theory of Competitive Advantage. *California Management Review*, Spring, 114-133.

Gurkov, I. (1998). Ownership and Control in Russian Privatised Companies: New Evidence from a Repeated Survey. *Communist Economies and Economic Transformation*, 10 (2), 259-70.

Gurkov, Igor B. and Asselsberg, G. (1995). Ownership and Control in Russian Privatized Companies: Evidence from a Survey. *Communist Economies and Economic Transformation*, 7 (2), 421-43.

Haakonsson, H. and Snehota, I. (1990): No Business is an Island: The Network Concept of Business Strategy. *Scandinavian Journal of Management*, 4 (3), 187-200.

Holden; Nigel J. (2000). Coping with Russia as a Bad Fit. In Crane, R.(ed.) *European Business Cultures*. London: Financial Times, Prentice Hall, 111-127.

Hooley, G. et al. (1996). Marketing Planning in Central and Eastern Europe. *Journal of Marketing Management*, 12, 69-82.

Huber, P. and Wörgötter, A. (1998). Political Survival or Entrepreneurial Development? Observations on Russian Business Networks. In Cohen, S., Schwartz, A. and Zysman, J. *The Tunnel at the end of the Light*. Berkley: University of California, 51-65.

Johanson, M., S. Kushch and Silver, L. (2000). Buyer-Seller Relationships in Transition: The Changing Business Environment in Russia. *Journal of East-West Business*, 6 (1), 35-56.

Johansson, J. K. and Nonaka, I. (1987). Market Research the Japanese Way. *Harvard Business Review*, no. 6, pp. 16-20.

Karpov, P. (1998). Kak vosstanovit' platezhesposobnost' rossiiskikh predpriatii. Rossiiskii ekonomicheskii zhurnal (4) 52-65.

Kharkhordin, O. and Gerber, T. P. (1994): Russian Directors Business Ethics: A Study of Industrial enterprises in St. Petersburg. *Europe-Asia Studies 46 (7)*, pp. 1075-1107.

Klayner, G. (1998). The Mechanism of Decision Making and Strategic Planning in Firms. *Questions of Economics*, (9) 46-65.

Kuada, J. and Sorensen, O. J. (1997). Planning Oriented versus Action Based Approach to the Internationalization of Firms. Working Paper No. 22. Aalborg: Center for International Studies, Aalborg University.

Kuznetsov, A. (1994). Economic Reforms in Russia: Enterprise Behavior as an Impediment to Change. *Europe-Asia Studies*, 46 (6).

Kuznetsov, A. and Kuznetsova, O. (1999). The State as a Shareholder: Responsibilities and Objectives. *Europe-Asia Studies*, 51 (3) 433-445.

Kuznetsova, O. and Kuznetsov, A. (1996). From a Socialist Enterprise to a Capitalist Firm: The Hazards of the Managerial Learning Curve. *Communist Economies & Economic Transformation*. 8 (4) 517-28.

Lethinen, U. (1996). Relationship Marketing Approaches in Changing Russian Markets. *Journal of East-West Business*. 1 (4) 35-49.

Lucas, S. and Maltsev, Y. (1996). The Development of Corporate Law in the Former Soviet Republics. *International and Comparative Law Quarterly, 45 (April), 365-391.*

Mitchell, R. K., Agle, B.R. and Wood, D.J. (1997). Toward a Theory of Stakeholder Identification and Salience: Defining the Principle of Who and What Really Counts. *Academy of Management Review*. 22 (4) 853-886.

OECD (1997). Globalisation and Small and Medium Enterprises. Vol. 1. Synthesis report. Paris: OECD

Paun, D.A. (1997). A Study of Best versus Average Buyer-Seller Relationships. *Journal of Business Research,* 39, issue 1, 13-21.

Popova, J. and Sorensen, O. J. (1996). Economic Reforms in Russia. A Network Perspective on the Firm's Reactions to the Reforms. Research Paper Series No. 2. International Business Economics. Aalborg: Center for International Studies, Aalborg University.

Popova, J. and Sorensen, O. J. (1997). The Emergence of Marketing Organization and Activity in Russian Firms. Proceedings from the Sixth International Conference on Marketing and Development. Black Sea University, Mangalia, Romania, July 1-4, 255-267.

Porter, M. E. (1985). *Competitive Advantage.* New York: Free Press.

Porter, M. E. (1980). *Competitive Strategy.* New York: Free Press.

Prahalad, C. K. and Hamal, G. (1990). The Core Competence of the Corporation. *Harvard Business Review,* May/June, 79-91.

Reekey, W. D. (1989). *Industrial Economics. A Critical Introduction to Corporate Firm in Europe and America.* Hants: Edward Elgar.

Richey, B. et al. (1999). Strategic Orientation of Russian Managers: Is the "New" Russian Firm Market Driven? *Journal of East-West Business,* 5 (1/2) 75-97.

Rose, R. (2000). Coping with Organizations: Networks of Russian Social Capital. Center for the Study of Public Policy (CSPP). Stratchdyde University, Glasgow. (http://www.socialcapital.strath.ac.uk/catalog31_0.html)

Salmi, A. (1996). Russian Networks in Transition. Implications for Managers. *Industrial Marketing Management,* 25 37-45.

Stern, L. W. and El-Ansary, A. I. (1988). *Marketing Channels,* 3rd edition. Englewood Cliffs, NJ.: Prentice Hall.

Vlachoutsicos, C. A. and Lawrence, P. R. (1996). How Managerial Learning can Assist Economic Transformation in Russia. *Organization Studies,* 17 (2), 311-325."

Zav'ialov, P. (1995). Rossiiskii rynok glazami marketologa. *Rossiiskii economicheskii zhurnal* (7) 44-54.

SUBMITTED: September 1999
FIRST REVISION: May 2000
SECOND REVISION: August 2000
ACCEPTED: August 2000

The Largest and Dominant Shareholders in the Russian Industry: Evidence of the Russian Economic Barometer Monitoring

Rostislav Kapelyushnikov

ABSTRACT. The paper analyses evolution of ownership structures and patterns of control at Russian privatized firms. The data are provided by three surveys, conducted by The Russian Economic Barometer in 1995, 1997 and 1999. According to results obtained, ownership profile of the Russian industry continues to be skewed in favor of insiders. However, in most cases the first largest shareholders are outside investors. Companies with medium concentration of shareholdings are more successful than companies with dispersed or highly concentrated ownership structure and firms under control of managers or financial outsiders outperform firms controlled by employees, non-financial outsiders or the state. *[Article copies available for a fee from The Haworth Document Delivery Service: 1-800-342-9678. E-mail address: <getinfo@haworthpressinc.com> Website: <http://www.HaworthPress.com> © 2001 by The Haworth Press, Inc. All rights reserved.]*

The study was supported by INTAS Project "Strategies for Firm Survival and Recovery," Ref No.96-109. The author is grateful to S. Aukutsionek, I. Filatochev and V. Zhukov for joint research and discussions on the problems of ownership and corporate governance in Russian, without which this paper could have hardly been written, and to O. Kuznetsova for valuable suggestions that helped substantially to improve the questionnaire.

[Haworth co-indexing entry note]: "The Largest and Dominant Shareholders in the Russian Industry: Evidence of the Russian Economic Barometer Monitoring." Kapelyushnikov, Rostislav. Co-published simultaneously in *Journal of East-West Business* (International Business Press, an imprint of The Haworth Press, Inc.) Vol. 6, No. 4, 2001, pp. 63-88; and: *Russian Corporations: The Strategies of Survival and Development* (ed: Andrei Kuznetsov) International Business Press, an imprint of The Haworth Press, Inc., 2001, pp. 63-88.

KEYWORDS. Russia, privatized firms, ownership structures, dominant shareholders, performance

INTRODUCTION

In the economic history of the mankind the Russian privatization experiment is unprecedented both in terms of the size of property transferred from the state sector into the hands of private owners and the pace at which this transfer took place. Surprisingly, so far there are quite few studies describing the evolution of the ownership profile of the Russian economy under transition. This is probably due to the informational vacuum in the post-privatization period rather than to the lack of interests on the part of researchers. Unfortunately, official statistics reflect the pattern of distribution of ownership across the main groups of shareholders only at the time of privatization. As a result there are no comprehensive data describing the redistribution of property rights at later stages.

In order to fill this gap the Russian Economic Barometer (REB) launched a special monitoring scheme covering the issues of ownership and corporate governance in Russian industry following the completion of the State Program of Mandatory Privatization. Two key issues were addressed by special surveys conducted by REB in 1995 and 1997. They were the dynamics of ownership in the post-privatization period and the impact of various patterns of control on firm performance, financial policy and investment activity. The analysis of the collected data showed that, first, the process of redistribution of shares was quite active in 1995-1997 and, second, in terms of firm behavior it did matter which categories of shareholders were dominating.

This paper analyses the evolution of ownership structures and patterns of control at Russian privatized firms in 1997-1999 through applying and further developing approaches that were offered in the previous REB publications (Aukutsionek, Kapeliushnikov and Zhukov, 1998; Aukutsionek, Filatochev, Kapeliushnikov and Zhukov, 1998).

CHARACTERISTICS OF THE DATA-SET

Three special surveys were conducted by REB at regular intervals in 1995, 1997 and 1999. The next survey is scheduled for 2001. The REB sample, despite its rather limited size, is fairly representative by its major structural characteristics (for comparisons of the REB sample with other samples and the whole population of Russian industrial firms, see Aukutsionek et al., 1998a; Aukutsionek et al., 1998b).

The first two surveys covered about 140 privatized firms across major branches and regions of Russia. In the last one about 160 valid responses were obtained. Moreover, about 50 respondents took part both in the 1995 and 1997 surveys (further, this panel will be abbreviated as *P5/7*) and about the same number took part both in the 1997 and 1999 surveys (*P7/9*).

In each survey, respondents provided information on distribution of equity capital of their firms among main groups of shareholders. Beside, in the 1999 survey, about two thirds of the respondents reported whatever category of owners their single largest shareholders belonged to and the size of the blocks of shares they possessed (in the previous surveys, these data were not collected). In addition, the surveys also contained respondent's forecasts of anticipated distribution in the next two years. In the 1995 survey, the expected distribution of shares was projected for the early 1997; in the 1997 survey, for the early 1999, and in the 1999 survey, for the early 2001. This allows to evaluate the directions and intensity of further probable changes in the ownership profile of the Russian industry.

TAXONOMY OF OWNERSHIP STRUCTURES AND PATTERNS OF CONTROL

Potential impact of the ownership factor on firms' behavior and performance follows from the fact that owners have formal rights to control their activities. As a result, the patterns of control prevailing in the economy and their effectiveness acquire great importance. However, in contrast to formal rights enjoyed by owners, the actual control over companies is not an observable variable. Only indirect evidence is available. In earlier studies two characteristics were identified as crucial in this respect (Short, 1994; Earle and Estrin, 1997).

The first is *the degree of concentration* of equity holdings. This was originally examined in the classic study by Berle and Means (1932), who famously revealed "the separation of ownership and control" in the modern public corporation. According to Berle and Means, dispersed shareholders are incapable of exercising effective control over manager's activity. On the contrary, concentration of the bulk of shares in the hands of a single owner or a group of owners helps to discipline their behavior. This implies that companies with dispersed shares would significantly differ performancewise from companies with highly concentrated equity holdings. The higher the concentration is, the more effective would be owner's control; the more their control is stringent, the better would be the performance.

Another aspect of the problem is different *identities* of owners (in particular, see Hansmann, 1996). The agency theory argues that various types of blockholders (even owning similar blocks of shares) may have quite different objective functions and face different costs of monitoring manager's activities (Shleifer and Vishny, 1996). This implies that behavior and performance of firms might vary reflecting dominance by different groups of shareholders.[1]

Virtually all studies on problems of corporate governance in the Russian economy under transition (including previous REB studies) focus on distribution of shares among *groups* of holders, leaving aside the issue of concentration of shares in the hands of *single* shareholders. This is partly due to non-availability of relevant data, and partly to the specifics of the Russian privatization which favored insiders. Consequently, all discussions on problems of corporate governance in Russia inevitably revolved around the issue of how stable this insider-skewed ownership structure would be.

The data of the 1999 REB survey provide an opportunity to follow a new approach and take into account concentration of equity in the hands of single owners. Information obtained allows us to construct three alternative classifications of firms reflecting their ownership structures and patterns of control. In a sense, these classifications are complementary to each other.

The first classification groups firms *by the size of the block of shares owned by a single largest shareholder*, be it an individual or a judicial person. Let us denote this single largest stake as *L1*. Depending on its magnitude, we can single out four classes of firms: those with low (*L1* is under 10%), medium (*L1* is from 10% to 20%), high (*L1* is from 20% to 50%) and super-high (*L1* is over 50%) ownership stakes in the hands of the first largest shareholder. In our sample each group consists of a roughly equal number of firms.

Following Earle and his co-authors (Earle, Estrin and Leschenko, 1996; see also: Earle, 1998), the second classification selects firms by *types of dominant shareholders*. Accordingly, we single out three large categories of firms: dominated by *insiders* (*IE*), dominated by *outsiders* (*OE*), and dominated by *the state* (*SE*). Insider controlled firms are further divided into dominated by managers (*ME*) and dominated by workers (*WE*). Firms under outsider's control are split into dominated by financial (*FE*) or non-financial outside shareholders (*NE*). Altogether, we have five types of firms: dominated by *managers* (ME), by *workers* (WE), by *financial outsiders* (*FE*), by *non-financial outsiders* (*NE*), and by *the state* (*SE*).[2]

A company was defined as dominated by insiders if their stake of shares was equal or larger than the stakes held by outsiders or the state. The insider-owned firm was classified as dominated by managers if their equity block was at least as large as controlled by workers. Otherwise it was classified as dominated by workers. Companies were identified as dominated by outsiders if their stake was larger than the stake of insiders and not less than the stake of the state. Likewise, the outsider-owned firm was qualified as dominated by financial outsiders if their block of equity was not smaller than that owned by non-financial outsiders; otherwise it was qualified as dominated by non-financial outsiders. When the majority of shares were owned by the state, firms were classified as state-dominated.

Finally, firms were classified by *the type of the first largest shareholder*. We shall denote these groups with the same abbreviations that are used for classes of firms with different types of dominant shareholders, adding mark (*): *IE*–firms with the first largest insider shareholder, ME*–firms with the first largest manager shareholder, WE*–firms with the first largest worker shareholder,* etc.

Taxonomies described above allow us to identify the categories of stockholders who are likely to have controlling powers and the means of control at their disposal. However, none of these typologies can reflect with absolute accuracy how effective control is actually distributed among different categories of owners. For instance, classification by size of maximum single block of shares leaves aside the issue of different identities of their holders. At the same time, classification by identity of the first largest shareholders does not take into account the size of their stakes that may be rather modest and for this reason insufficient to establish effective control. As for classification by types of dominant shareholders, it ignores the "free rider problem" and difficulties involved in reconciling conflicting interests within each particular group of owners. Even if a certain category of owners holds the bulk of shares in a company stock, diffusion of shares among numerous small holders would increase costs of concerted action and make them passive owners (this situation is most expectable at firms dominated by workers or individual outside shareholders). Nonetheless, using these three classifications concurrently, it is possible to obtain a fairly complete and detailed picture of what kind of ownership structures and patterns of control have emerged in the Russian industry and in what ways they might evolve in the nearest future.

BASIC CHARACTERISTICS
OF THE CURRENT DISTRIBUTION OF SHARES

Table 1 summarizes the basic findings of the REB monitoring in 1995-1999. While the results of consequent surveys are not directly comparable, the revealed general patterns are close enough. It is a well known fact that first "spontaneous" privatization, based on leasing out state-owned firms with an option of buy-out, and later mandatory privatization helped to concentrate the bulk of equity in the hands of managers and workers. REB surveys confirm that the initial distribution of shares was, indeed, clearly in favor of insiders.

TABLE 1. Ownership Profile of the Russian Industry According to REB Monitoring, 1995-2001 (%)*

Categories of shareholders	1995	1997	1999	2001 (forecast)
Insiders, total	**54.8**	**52.1**	**46.2**	**45.5**
Managers	11.2	15.1	14.7	18.2
Workers	43.6	37.0	31.5	27.2
Outsiders, total	**35.2**	**38.8**	**42.4**	**44.9**
Non-financial outsiders, total	25.9	28.5	32.0	31.9
Outside individuals	10.9	13.9	18.5	16.9
Other firms	15.0	14.6	13.5	15.0
Financial outsiders, total	9.3	10.3	10.4	13.0
The state	**9.1**	**7.4**	**7.1**	**6.4**
Other shareholders	**0.9**	**1.7**	**4.3**	**3.2**
Grand total	**100**	**100**	**100**	**100**

*136 respondents took part in the 1995 survey; 135, in the 1997 survey; 156, in the 1999 survey.
In 1999, 94 respondents gave their forecasts of the anticipated ownership structure for 2001.

Surveys also indicate that this insider-skewed ownership profile was kept over the whole post-privatization period. What is more, according to forecasts made by REB respondents, the bulk of equity may belong to insiders even in 2001 (see corresponding data in the last column of Table 1).

The latest REB survey gives a more comprehensive picture of the current distribution of shares (Table 2). According to its findings, in 1999, only one out of 20 industrial firms was free from insider ownership. Managers and workers remained the largest groups of shareholders: their combined share was 46.2% of total stock. Workers held 31.5% of shares, managers 13.6% and the residual 1.1% were held by subsidiaries established by firms.[3] Meanwhile, in the early 1999, outsider ownership was already quite common: it was absent only in one firm out of ten. However, there was a very large number of firms (80-90%) that had no banks, investment funds, holding companies or foreign investors among their owners. At the same time, four firms out of five had individual outside shareholders. This proliferation of individual ownership is a new phenomenon not observed in earlier studies, including previous REB surveys.

The cumulative stake of outside owners was a little smaller than the cumulative stake of insiders (42.4%). Interestingly, it mostly belonged to non-financial outsiders (32.0%), while financial outsiders had only 10.4%. Average blocks of shares held by banks, investment funds, holding companies, or foreign investors were no larger than 3-4%. As for non-financial outsiders, the stake of outside individuals looked unexpectedly large: 18.5%, or almost 1.5 times as high as the stake of "other firms" (13.5%). The state kept 7.1% of eq-

TABLE 2. Ownership Structure of the REB Respondent Firms, 1999

Groups of shareholders	Average shareholdings (unweighted), %[1]	Average shareholdings (weighted), %[2]	Distribution of firms by size of blocks of shares owned by particular categories of holders, %[2]						
			0%	0-10%	10-20%	20-30%	30-40%	> 40%	Total
Insiders, total	46.2 (30.3)	43.3	4.5	10.2	10.3	12.2	8.3	54.5	100
Managers+[3]	14.7 (18.9)	10.3	12.8	51.3	14.1	7.1	4.5	10.3	100
Managers	13.6 (18.1)	9.4	13.5	53.2	14.8	5.1	3.8	9.6	100
Subsidiaries established by firms	1.1 (4.8)	0.9	91.0	4.5	2.6	0.7	0.6	0.6	100
Workers	31.5 (24.2)	33.0	7.7	16.6	14.7	16.7	13.5	30.8	100
Outsiders, total	42.4 (28.9)	47.1	8.3	12.8	7.1	8.3	13.5	50.0	100
Non-financial outsiders, total	32.0 (27.0)	33.8	14.8	17.9	9.6	9.6	13.5	34.6	100
Outsiders individuals	18.5 (21.5)	16.5	21.8	31.4	15.4	7.0	10.9	13.5	100
State-owned firms	0.9 (5.9)	1.0	96.8	0.7	0.6	1.3	0	0.6	100
Privatized firms	6.6 (17.0)	5.2	78.2	7.7	1.3	2.6	2.5	7.7	100
Private firms	6.0 (14.5)	11.1	76.9	7.7	1.9	5.1	2.6	5.8	100
Financial outsiders, total	10.4 (20.9)	13.3	65.4	9.6	7.1	5.1	2.6	10.2	100
Commercial banks	1.0 (5.2)	1.4	91.0	5.8	1.9	0.7	0	0.6	100
Investment funds	3.9 (12.0)	3.5	80.8	8.3	4.5	3.2	1.3	1.9	100
Holding, investment and insurance companies	3.5 (12.4)	4.3	87.2	3.8	2.6	1.3	1.3	3.8	100
Foreign investors	2.0 (12.0)	4.1	96.8	0	0	0	0.6	2.6	100
State, total	7.1 (17.6)	6.4	78.2	3.8	6.4	3.2	1.3	7.1	100
Federal and regional property funds	5.8 (15.9)	5.7	80.8	3.2	7.7	3.2	0	5.1	100
Regional and local administrations	1.3 (7.8)	0.7	95.5	1.9	0.7	0	0	1.9	100
Other and non-identified shareholders	4.3 (15.6)	3.2	87.2	3.8	2.6	0.6	1.3	4.5	100
Grand total	100	100	–	–	–	–	–	–	–

[1] Standard deviations in parentheses.
[2] Average shares in stock, weighted by firm size.
[3] Total share in stock owned by managers and subsidiaries established by firms.

uity of which 5.8% belonged to the Federal or regional property funds and 1.3% to regional or local administrations.

Table 2 also presents average stakes belonging to various groups of shareholders, weighted by firm size (weights were calculated from numbers of employees). It shows that shareholdings of managers and individuals were relatively larger at smaller firms. By contrast, "other firms" and financial outsiders appeared more often among shareholders of large firms.

However, disparities between weighted and non-weighted estimates don't look very significant, and this confirms that firms of different size had a more or less similar distribution of equity interests among major groups of shareholders.

As for another basic characteristic of ownership structure, *the concentration of equity holdings,* the general bias of Russian privatization in favor of insiders might give grounds to two conflicting hypotheses. (1) The bulk of the stock was initially distributed among a large number of employees. It is possible to expect, therefore, that the level of ownership concentration should be relatively low. (2) Individual outside investors have no incentives to buy shares of firms in which the interests of minority shareholders are not respected, or which are mostly loss-makers, or do not provide reliable information on their financial conditions, etc. In such a situation, it would be reasonable to expect that the bulk of shares would be concentrated in the hands of few large owners. The 1999 REB survey clearly supports the second hypothesis. On average the single largest stake amounted to 32% in the REB sample, indicating that the ownership structure in the Russian industry is highly concentrated.

DYNAMICS OF REDISTRIBUTION

In previous REB studies based on the results of 1995 and 1997 surveys, we traced main routes of redistribution of shares in the post-privatization period: from the state to non-state owners, from insiders to outsiders, and from workers to managers. We recorded some disturbing symptoms hampering the formation of a workable corporate governance system. Most noticeably, banks and investment funds that were expected to become "effective owners" saw their shareholdings shrinking. It can be seen from *P7/9* panel that these tendencies continued in 1997-1999 (Table 3). There was further weakening of financial outsiders. At the same time an almost two-fold increase in the stake of individual outside investors from 10.4% to 19.5% came as a surprise.

The gross intensity of redistribution can be measured with an integral indicator *m* computed from the formula:

$$m = 1/2 \ \Sigma |d_i(t) - d_i(t{-}2)|,$$

where $d_i(t)$ и $d_i(t{-}2)$ are average equity stakes belonging to an *i* group of shareholders at present *(t)* and two years earlier *(t–2),* respectively. A multiplier 1/2 is introduced to avoid double counting, since the sum of positive changes is equal to the sum of negative changes by definition. Indicator *m* shows what

TABLE 3. Changes in Ownership Structure of the REB Respondent Firms, 1997-1999 (%) [1]

Groups of shareholders	Average shareholdings	
	1997	1999
Insiders, total	**59.7**	**55.3**
Managers + [2]	*18.0*	*20.1*
Workers	*41.7*	*35.2*
Outsiders, total	**30.5**	**35.7**
Non-financial outsiders, total	*20.5*	*28.1*
Outsiders individuals	10.4	19.5
Other firms	10.1	8.6
Financial outsiders, total	*10.0*	*7.6*
Banks	0.9	0.6
Investment funds	2.9	1.1
Holding & other companies	3.9	3.5
Foreign investors	2.3	2.3
The state	**9.7**	**8.3**
Other shareholders	**0.1**	**0.5**
Total	**100**	**100**

[1] The Table is based on a sub-sample of 43 firms that took part both in the 1997 and 1999 REB surveys.
[2] Total share in stock owned by managers and subsidiaries established by firms.

part of share capital was redistributed among main groups of shareholders within two year intervals.[4]

According to REB estimates, in 1995-1997, intensity of inter-group "migration" of shares reached 17% (Aukutsionek et al., 1998a; Aukutsionek et al., 1998b). In 1997-1999, it was somewhat lower at about 12%. A tentative conclusion inspired by these data is that, although in 1997-1999 the rate of ownership redistribution in the Russian industry declined as compared with the first post-privatization years, it still remained quite substantial.

WHAT PATTERNS OF CONTROL PREVAIL?

Wide diversity of intra-firm ownership profiles inevitably implies variability of patterns of control. It may be assumed that the forms and efficiency of control would vary depending on the size of the single largest blocks of shares, the identity of its owners and the type of dominant shareholders (see Section 2). Comparing groups of firms that differ in these dimensions we can assess, first, the incidence of prevailing forms of control, second, specificity of ownership profiles within particular groups of firms, and third, interrelation between characteristics that shape existing patterns of control. In other words, how large are "the zones of control" by leading categories of owners in the Russian industry? What is the stake of shares required to really influence the process of decision-making? How is control exercised by different categories of stakeholders relates to concentration of equity holdings?

Incidence of a Particular Form of Control

(a) Distribution of surveyed firms *by concentration of shareholdings* is presented in Chart 1. In 19% of them, the level of concentration was low (*L1* under 10%); at 21% it was medium (*L1* ranging from 10 to 20%); 25% it was high (*L1* in the range of 20-50%); and at 22% it was super-high (the single largest shareholder owned controlling blocks). The remaining 13% of respondents reported that they knew neither the size of maximum block of shares nor who its owner was. Therefore, in half industrial firms the first largest shareholder had substantial blocks of equity capital, big enough to really influence decision- making and to have interest in efficient monitoring of manager's behavior.

(b) To describe distribution of Russian industrial firms *by categories of dominant shareholders* we can use findings of all three surveys. Although the composition of respondents did not remain the same, they still allow us to record some general trends in the evolution of ownership structures and patterns of control. As follows from Table 4, the Russian industry entered the post-privatization period with an obvious prevalence of insider's control. The portion of workers-dominated firms was particularly high. However, soon the workers' "zone of control" started to shrink, while the "zone of control" of managers and non-financial outsiders began to expand. Surprisingly, the fraction of firms dominated by financial outsiders stayed almost unchanged. It is significant that these conclusions are supported by data of our panels, *P5/7* and *P7/9*.

In 1999, the composition of surveyed firms appeared as follows (see Table 4): insiders dominated in 48% of them, outsides in 45% and the state in 7%. Workers and non-financial outsiders were dominant owners of every third firm, managers of every seventh and financial outsiders of every tenth. As we can see, while insider's firms remain the most common type, almost half of firms have already passed under the control of outside investors. Nevertheless, if the forecasts made by firm managers in the early 1999 are going to come true, even as late as 2001, the major part of the Russian industry would be still controlled by insiders.

(c) Distribution of firms by identity of their *first largest shareholder* gives the following results: insiders control 27% of all firms, outsiders 60% and the state 13%. In other words, following this approach, by early 1999 most indus-

CHART 1. Distribution of Firms by Size of Single Largest Blocks of Shares, 1999

	Stakes of the single largest shareholders as % of total firm equity				
	0-10%	10-20%	20-50%	50-100%	unknown
Percentage of firms, %	19	21	25	22	13

Note: The Chart is based on sub-sample of 117 firms that responded to questions on size of stakes owned by the first largest shareholders and their identity.

TABLE 4. Distribution of the REB Respondent Firms by Categories of Dominant Shareholders, 1995-2001 (%)

Groups of firms with different types of dominant shareholders	1995	1997	1999	2001 (forecast).
IE	59	53	48	49
ME	7	11	15	21
WE	52	42	33	28
OE	36	39	45	46
NE	27	28	34	31
FE	9	11	11	15
SE	5	8	7	5
Total sample	100	100	100	100

trial firms had already gone under the rule of outsiders, while only a quarter remained under control of insiders. As could be anticipated, the number of firms controlled by outside individuals and workers was very small (for instance, only one respondent reported that an employee owned the largest block of shares). This means that in the majority of firms in which the maximum *cumulative* blocks of shares were owned by outsider individuals or workers, the maximum *single* blocks belonged to owners representing other categories of shareholders. In sum, the classification by identity of the first largest shareholder reveals a significant increase in the share of firms controlled by managers (by 12%), financial outsiders (10%) or the state (by 7%) in comparison with the classification in terms of dominant groups of owners (see the last line in Table 7).

Specifics of Intra-Group Composition of Shareholdings

(a) Table 5 displays ownership profiles of firms that differed *by size of single largest blocks of shares*. It shows that workers' shareholdings monoto-

TABLE 5. Ownership Profiles of Firms with Different Size of Single Largest Blocks of Shares, 1999 (%) [1]

Categories of shareholders	Groups of firms by size of single largest blocks of shares				All firms
	0-10%	10-20%	20-50%	over 50%	
Insiders	66	52	44	16	44
Managers + [2]	*12*	*18*	*20*	*5*	*14*
Workers	*54*	*33*	*25*	*10*	*30*
Outsiders	33	41	47	54	44
Non-financial outsiders	*31*	*29*	*35*	*34*	*32*
Outsiders individuals	23	19	16	13	17
Other firms	8	10	19	21	15
Financial outsiders	*2*	*12*	*12*	*20*	*12*
The state	1	6	3	18	7
Other shareholders	0	1	5	12	5
Total	100	100	100	100	100

[1] The Table is based on the data on 100 firms with identified first largest shareholders.
[2] Total share in stock owned by managers and subsidiaries established by firms.

nously declined along with the increase in *L1*. In the case of managers, the relationship turns out to be non-linear: their stake was smaller in two polar groups, namely, those with the highest and the lowest concentration of equity holdings. Finally, there was a negative correlation between *L1* and the stake of outside individuals and a positive one between *L1* and stakes belonging to such categories of owners as "other firms," financial outsiders and the state.

(b) What stake should a group of shareholders have in order to bargain for the status of a *dominant owner?* Chart 2 provides answer to this question. According to the 1999 survey, the mean stake owned by dominant shareholders of different types varied from 52% in the case of *ME* to 64% in the case of *FE*. Similar results were obtained by the 1997 survey. In other words, groups of shareholders have to accumulate very large blocks of shares, usually larger than controlling interest, to gain a dominant position. This confirms the conclusion of previous REB studies that high concentration of equity holdings in the hands of dominant shareholders creates an insurmountable barrier to any other categories wishing to challenge their control over a firm (Aukutsionek et al., 1998a; Aukutsionek et al., 1998b).

(c) Let us turn to ownership profiles of firms with different types of *the first largest shareholders.* As follows from Table 6, the mean size of blocks of shares owned by the largest shareholder varied significantly depending on their identity. For insiders it never exceeded 20%, while for outsiders it

CHART 2. Average Stakes Owned by Dominant Shareholders as Depending on Their Types, 1997-1999 (%)

	Groups of firms by types of dominant shareholders				
	ME	WE	NE	FE	SE
1997	53	59	62	57	59
1999	52	59	62	64	62

TABLE 6. Stakes Owned by the Single Largest Shareholders as Depending on Their Identity, 1999 (%) [1]

Groups of firms by type of the first largest shareholders	Average stakes owned by the first largest shareholders	Blocks of shares owned by all holders of the same category as the first largest owner	Stake of the first largest shareholder as % of block of shares owned by all holders of the same category
(1)	(2)	(3)	(4)
IE*	16.2	78.1	21
ME*	16.7	34.5	48
WE*	4.9	63.0	8
OE*	35.6	62.1	57
NE*	35.1	58.7	60
Firms with outside individuals as the first largest owners	29.7	44.1	67
Firms with "other firms" as the first largest owners	37.0	43.9	84
FE*	36.3	43.8	83
SE*	42.5	44.9	95
Firms with "other shareholders" as the first largest owners	54.1	54.1	100

[1] The Table is based on the data on 100 firms with identified first largest shareholders.

reached 30-40% and for the state it increased to 40-50%. Interestingly, for different groups of outsiders it was quite similar from about 30% for outside individuals, banks and investment funds to about 40% for "other firms", holding companies and foreign investors. What fractions of cumulative blocks of shares held by certain groups of owners are concentrated in the hands of the single largest blockholders from those groups? The largest blockholders among managers and outside individuals held 48-67% of cumulative blocks of shares belonging to these groups of owners (Table 6). This implies that they may face serious problems in forming coalitions within their own groups. In other groups, a similar indicator amounted to 83-95% proving that the largest owners commanded virtually whole blocks of shares held by their groups.

Correlation Between Characteristics Shaping Particular Patterns of Control

(a) What types of dominant owners are most common in firms with high and low *L1*? According to Table 7, two thirds of firms with low concentration of shares in the hands of the single largest holder (*L1* not above 10%) and none with super-high concentration (*L1* over 50%) were dominated by workers. On the contrary, no participant of the first group and about a quarter of participants in the second group were dominated by financial outsiders or by the state. A sizeable part of firms in two central groups (with *L1* in the range between 10% and 50%) were dominated by managers, while dominance of non-financial outsiders was more frequent among firms with high and super-high *L1*.

(b) In terms of classification by the identity of the first largest shareholder results turn out to be slightly different. Available data (Table 7) seem to support the view that dispersed ownership commonly associated with control by insiders while more concentrated ownership with control by outsiders. For instance, managers held maximum stakes at 60% firms with *L1* under 10%, while at 50-80% firms with higher levels of concentration the first largest shareholder was an outsider. Apparently, in accumulating large blocks of shares managers, due to limited access to financial resources, confront with more serious difficulties than outside investors.

(c) Finally, our analysis shows that there is a fairly high degree of conformity between the classification of firms *by dominant types of shareholders* and their classification *by types of the first largest shareholder*. For instance, it follows from Table 8 that in the majority of firms dominated by certain groups of

TABLE 7. Distribution of Firms with Different Size of Maximum Block of Shares by Types of Dominant/Largest Shareholders, 1999 (%)[1]

Groups of firms by size of maximum block of shares (*L1*)	Groups of firms by types of dominant shareholders							Total/ total*
	IE/IE*			OE/OE*			SE/SE*	
	Total	of which		Total	of which			
		ME/ME*	WE/WE*		NE/NE*	FE/FE*		
0-10%	68/65	5/60	63/5	32/35	32/25	0/10	0/5	100/100
10-20%	62/24	17/24	45/0	38/47	29/14	8/33	0/29	100/100
20-50%	38/13	24/18	14/0	62/78	48/52	14/26	0/4	100/100
over 50%	8/4	8/14	0/0	64/70	36/39	28/31	24/26	100/100
All firms which provided assessments of *L1*	44/27	14/26	30/1	50/60	37/36	13/24	6/13	100/100

[1] The Table is based on the data on 100 firms with identified first largest shareholders

TABLE 8. Distribution of Firms with Different Dominant Shareholders by Types of the First Largest Shareholders, 1999 (%) [1]

Groups of firms by types of dominant shareholders	Groups of firms by types of the first largest shareholders								
	IE*			OE*			SE*	Un-identi-fied	Total
	Total	of which		Total	of which				
		ME*	WE*		NE*	FE*			
IE	49	47	2	28	15	13	8	15	100
ME	75	75	0	12	6	6	0	13	100
WE	39	36	3	36	19	17	8	17	100
OE	2	2	0	83	53	30	6	9	100
NE	2	2	0	78	68	10	7	13	100
FE	0	0	0	100	0	100	0	0	100
SE	0	0	0	0	0	0	75	25	100

[1] The Table is based on sub-sample of 117 firms that responded to questions on size of stakes owned by the first largest shareholders and their identity.

shareholders the single largest blocks were also held by members of the same groups. The only exception is *WE*, since, as it was noticed, there were virtually no largest shareholders among employees. This means that, with the exception of *WE*, classification by categories of dominant shareholders is a sufficiently reliable source of information about the types of owners exerting actual control over particular firms.

IMPACT OF OWNERSHIP STRUCTURES AND PATTERNS OF CONTROL ON BEHAVIOR AND PERFORMANCE OF FIRMS

Firm Performance and Concentration of Ownership

According to Table 9, in terms of performance, firms with medium concentration of equity in the hands of the single largest shareholder (*L1* ranging from 10 to 20%) were in the most favorable position. Compared to other groups, their order-book level was 9-16% higher, the rate of capacity utilization was 9-15% higher and the rate of labor utilization was 4-11% higher. In this group the fraction of firms that assessed their current financial condition as "bad" was about half as small as in other groups. Equally, the proportion of loss-making products in total output was much lower, about 10% against 14-26% in other groups. The share of loss-making firms was also minimal at 22%. In 1999 members of this group maintained the same stock of production capacities as in the previous year. Their net job losses were also insignificant at no more than 1.4% while they paid higher wages.

TABLE 9. Performance of Firms with Different Size of Single Largest Blocks of Shares, 1999 (%)

Indicators (average values)	Groups of firms by size of single largest blocks of shares			
	0-10%	10-20%	20-50%	over 50%
Order-book level[1]	67	82	73	66
Capacity utilization rate[1]	58	67	55	53
Labor utilization rate[1]	82	86	78	75
Share of barter in sales	38	42	52	53
Production capacities as compared to the previous year[2]	−5	0	−10	−5
Percentage of firms in "bad" financial condition	63	33	68	72
Share of loss-making products in total output	14.1	9.8	18.7	25.7
Percentage of loss-making firms according to financial balance of the last six months	23	22	52	52
Change in employment in the previous 12 months[3]	−1.6	−1.4	−8.6	−0.2
Separation rate[3]	14.4	19.0	17.2	18.6
Hiring rate[3]	12.8	17.6	18.6	18.4
% of lay-offs in total separations	12	15	15	10
Share of employees with no remuneration in money for the last month	14	15	19	19
Average wages, rubles	1086	1121	813	874
Average number of employees, persons	593	875 [4]	751	494

[1] As of February 1999, % of the normal level taken as 100%.
[2] % of production capacities a year ago.
[3] % of total employees.
[4] Excluding one extra-large firm (14000 employees) that falls into this group.

The group of firms with the lowest level of concentration of equity holdings was nearest to the leading group and firms with high *L1* ranked below them (see Table 9). Surprisingly, firms with maximum accumulation of equity in the hands of the single largest shareholders appeared to be disadvantaged the most. They were at the bottom of the ranking in terms of the level of orders, capacity and labor utilization. Also they resorted to barter more actively. Two thirds of these firms assessed their current financial condition as "bad," and a quarter of their output was loss-making. Wages were quite low, and their workforce suffered most from wage arrears. In the month preceding the survey, every fifth worker received no remuneration in money. Despite these facts, employment reduction was minimal in this group, which may be a sign that these firms were quite inclined to hoard "superfluous workers."

Our conclusion that correlation between the concentration of equity holdings and firms' performance is non-linear is not dissimilar to certain findings obtained for managerial ownership in mature market economies (see: Morck,

Shleifer and Vishny, 1988) (6). At the same time our analysis provided some surprises. The greatest is the fact that the poorest performance is displayed by firms that have more than a half of their stock owned by a single largest share-holder. This is obviously a challenge to the notion widely accepted by Russian researchers that there is no better way to create an "effective owner" then to concentrate controlling interest in the hands of one shareholder.

Firm Performance and the Identity of Largest Owners

By the level of received orders, capacity and labor utilization rates the best performance was exhibited by firms whose largest owners were managers (*ME**) (see Table 10). These firms were less involved in barter deals and more often assessed their financial condition as "normal" or "good". Loss-making products amounted to less than 10% of their output against 20-25% in other groups. In the *ME** group, only every fourth firm was a loss-maker, while in

TABLE 10. Performance of Firms with Different Types of the First Largest Shareholders, 1999 (%)

Indicators (average values)	Groups of firms by type of the first largest shareholders*				
	ME*	NE*	FE*	SE*	Unidentified
Order-book level[1]	85	67	70	77	69
Capacity utilization rate[1]	64	57	59	52	50
Labor utilization rate[1]	86	78	81	75	64
Share of barter in sales	40	45	49	64	51
Production capacities as compared to the previous year[2]	−1	−7	−9	−2	−4
Percentage of firms in "bad" financial condition	52	68	52	77	71
Share of loss-making products in total output	9.0	18.7	19.7	23.3	23.2
Percentage of loss-making firms according to financial balance of the last six months	23	44	43	50	53
Change in employment in the previous 12 months[3]	+3.8	−2.6	−9.6	+2.0	−5.8
Separation rate[3]	12.6	24.2	24.4	13.0	26.2
Hiring rate[3]	16.4	21.6	14.8	15.0	20.4
% of lay-offs in total separations	8	9	27	8	27
Share of employees with no remuneration in money for the last month	14	23	14	15	20
Average wages, rubles	1145	914	909	878	889
Average number of employees, persons	544	946	963	762	511

* Data on WE* with workers as the first largest shareholders are omitted for the group was presented by a single firm.
[1] As of February 1999, % of the normal level taken as 100%.
[2] % of production capacities a year ago.
[3] % of total employees.

other groups every second was. *ME** type firms managed to stabilize production, create new jobs and pay the highest wages.

The *FE** group with the single largest stakes belonging to banks, investment funds, holding companies or foreign investors, were less successful than *ME** but outperformed other groups on most parameters. At the same time these firms have displayed the highest rates of capacity "shedding" (-9%) and job losses (-9.6%), which may be seen as an evidence that they were more actively engaged in restructuring.

NE* and *SE** type firms were in a much more distressed situation. They had lower rates of capacity and labor utilization (52-57% and 75-78% respectively), two thirds of them assessed their financial condition as "bad," and every second respondent was a loss-maker. Firms in which the state played the role of largest shareholder (*SE**) were inclined more than others to resort to barter, while the share of loss-making products in total output was particularly high. As for the firms with non-financial outsiders as their first largest owners (*NE**), their employees suffered most from delays in wage payments: in the month preceding the survey, about a quarter of them received no remuneration in money at all. At the same time, these groups differed in one important respect. While *NE** type firms were more or less active in disposing of excess production capacities and labor, firms in the *SE** group maintained their capacities at a virtually unchanged level and increased their employment despite the fact that their capacities were underutilized by one-half and their work force was underutilized by one-fourth. It appears that old "non-market" patterns of behavior have been preserved mostly in this group.

Firms *with non-identified first largest shareholders* were also in visible distress. They lagged behind other groups on such performance indicators as capacities and labor utilization rates, the percentage of profit-makers and ability to pay wages on time. By other indicators, they share the lowest positions with *SE**. The fact that respondents have no information on their largest shareholders is indirect evidence of vagueness and non-transparency of ownership structures in a certain number of firms. This allows us to conclude that in transition economies, attenuation of property rights may be no less damaging for the efficiency of a firm than concentration of the bulk of equity in the hands of shareholders who are disinterested or unable to maximize firms' market value (see Kapeliushnikov, 1997).

As it follows from Table 7, the group with highly concentrated ownership was composed mainly of firms whose largest shareholders were non-financial outsiders or the state. Meanwhile, we have established that in terms of performance, *NE** and *SE** lose by a wide margin to *ME** or *FE**. Hence, it becomes clear why firms with super-high concentration of ownership were commonly inferior in performance: *in many cases super-high stakes belong to the least ef-*

ficient categories of owners. In conceptual terms this conclusion implies that arguments in favor of concentration of equity capital which do not take into account the identity of the largest shareholders are likely to prove misleading.

Firm Performance and Dominant Categories of Shareholders

The contrasts that were revealed while comparing firms with different largest shareholders become even more striking when firms are classified by category of dominant shareholders (Table 11). Previous REB studies disclosed a positive correlation between dominance of managers or financial outsiders and the performance of firms (Aukutsionek et al., 1998a; Aukutsionek et al., 1998b). The 1999 survey brought a new verification of this fact: firms controlled by managers or financial outsiders demonstrated the best performance (*FE* were inferior to *ME*, but in most cases only slightly).

Firms dominated by workers (*WE*) or non-financial outsiders (*NE*) were in a much worse situation: 60-70% assessed their financial condition as "bad," and

TABLE 11. Performance of Firms with Different Types of Dominant Shareholders, 1999 (%)

Indicators (average values)	Groups of firms by types of dominant shareholders				
	ME	WE	NE	FE	SE
Order-book level[1]	83	76	67	85	101
Capacity utilization rate[1]	65	56	51	64	45
Labor utilization rate[1]	84	79	78	82	64
Share of barter in sales	39	42	50	45	70
Production capacities as compared to the previous year[2]	−4	−4	−7	−5	−2
Percentage of firms in "bad" financial condition	43	61	71	56	90
Share of loss-making products in total output	11.1	18.3	17.7	22.0	37.8
Percentage of loss-making firms according to financial balance of the last six months.	23	40	45	38	82
Change in employment in the previous 12 months[3]	−2.4	−4.8	−6.8	−3.6	+1.2
Separation rate[3]	23.0	19.8	27.2	22.4	21.6
Hiring rate[3]	20.6	15.0	20.4	18.8	22.8
% of lay-offs in total separations	10	18	15	23	9
Share of employees with no remuneration in money for the last month	0	17	18	19	37
Average wages, rubles	992	1022	863	1112	761
Average number of employees, persons	462	745	851	919	429

[1] As of February 1999, % of the normal level taken as 100%.
[2] % of the volume of production capacities a year ago.
[3] % of total employees.

almost every second firm was a loss-maker. It is interesting to note that, as a rule, firms with dominant non-financial outsiders were inferior even in comparison with companies dominated by workers. It is possible that equity held by individual shareholders as the prevailing sub-type of non-financial outsiders is in fact as a shield to protect incumbent managers from intrusion of financial outsiders, rather than a tool to discipline their behavior (Aukutsionek et al., 1998a; Aukutsionek et al., 1998b). Russian managers usually monitor very closely any changes in the composition of shareholders of their firms. There are good reasons to believe that individual shareholders are typically either proxy agents for incumbent managers or retired employees. Obviously, this peculiar form of individual ownership is likely to help the "entrenchment" of managers rather than restrain their opportunistic behavior, which provides a sensible explanation for the poor performance of firms with dominant non-financial outsiders (*NE*).

Finally, firms dominated by the state (*SE*) underperformed as compared with all other groups. The percentage of barter in their transactions reached 70%, and in the month preceding the survey, every third worker had no remuneration in money. Nevertheless, they continued to keep their capacities almost unchanging. They even increased the number of employees. Obviously, *SEs* face the greatest barriers to restructuring.

IMPACT OF OWNERSHIP STRUCTURES AND PATTERNS OF CONTROL ON FINANCIAL AND INVESTMENT POLICIES

Let us compare the financial and investment policies of firms with different concentration of equity capital in the hands of the single largest shareholder (Table 12). In general, firms with medium concentration of ownership (*L1* ranging from 10 to 20%) look better than all others. Their bank debt was relatively small; their capital investments were declining at a slower rate than that in groups with more concentrated shareholdings; they fared better in managing investment plans (at the same time, firms without any investment plans were more frequent in this group). It is worth noting that the group with the dispersed equity ownership had the lowest share of external sources in capital investment, while the group with the most concentrated equity ownership had the highest. However, intensive external financing in the latter group appears to be based on non-market sources, such as subsidies and soft credit. Characteristically, anticipated interest rates on bank loans were much lower in this group than in any other.

Firms with different types of largest or dominant shareholders demonstrated even sharper contrasts in financial and investment policies. According

TABLE 12. Characteristics of Financial and Investment Policies of Firms with Different Size of Single Largest Blocks of Shares, 1999 (%)

Indicators (average values)	Groups of firms by size of single largest blocks of shares			
	0-10%	10-20%	20-50%	over 50%
Indebtedness to commercial banks [1]	77	67	71	111
Shares of firms not going to make bank borrowing in the next 3 months	45	38	31	48
Anticipated interest rates on credits to be received in the next 3 months	48	43	42	29
Volume of capital investments [2]	55	50	39	33
% of investments financed from:				
external sources [3]	0	18	14	23
internal sources [3]	100	82	86	77
% of investment into:				
machinery and equipment [3]	84	72	69	82
buildings and structures [3]	16	28	31	18
% of investment into:				
expansion of capacities [3]	15	24	31	24
maintenance and modernization [3]	85	76	69	76
Share of firms without investment plans	27	38	31	32
% of fulfillment of investment plans in the previous 6 months	49	65	50	28
The highest interest rate to be afforded by firms for investment loans	9	10	14	10

[1] As of February 1999, % of the normal level taken as 100%.
[2] Volume of investments (in real terms) in the previous 6 months, as % of the volume of investments in the same period a year ago.
[3] % of total investments.

to Table 13, the great majority of firms had lower indebtedness to banks than the level that they consider "normal," regardless of the type of dominant shareholders. The only exception was the *SE* group, with indebtedness to banks more than twice as high as this level. *WE* and *FE* occupied the opposite ends of the scale, demonstrating the greatest "appetite" for credit resources. Correspondingly, every second *SE* but only every fourth *ME* and *FE* had no intentions to borrow in the coming quarter. Annual interest rates on loans anticipated by different groups in the early 1999 were almost identical, at 35-40%. Again, the only exception was the *SE* group, which expected to obtain loans at 20%, almost half the going rate, probably because they had access to the sources of "soft" credit.

The constant fall in production investment has plagued the Russian economy ever since the market reforms started. *MEs* were probably most successful in resisting this trend. Their investment reduced in real terms by less than

TABLE 13. Characteristics of Financial and Investment Policies of Firms with Different Types of Dominant Shareholders, 1999 (%)

Indicators (average values)	Groups of firms by types of dominant shareholders				
	ME	WE	NE	FE	SE
Indebtedness to commercial banks[1]	68	47	92	53	213
Shares of firms not going to make bank borrowings in the next 3 months	22	43	42	25	55
Anticipated interest rates on credits to be received in the next 3 months	36	37	36	38	20
Volume of capital investments [2]	51	36	37	32	30
% of investments financed from: external sources [3]	20	12	18	23	45
internal sources [3]	80	88	82	77	55
% of investment into: machinery and equipment [3]	84	68	77	92	82
buildings and structures [3]	16	32	23	8	18
% of investment into: expansion of capacities [3]	49	29	18	4	15
maintenance and modernization [3]	51	71	82	96	85
Share of firms without investment plans	26	29	40	25	55
% of fulfillment of investment plans in the previous 6 months	52	46	40	55	30
The highest interest rate to be afforded by firms for investment loans	14	11	9	16	5

[1] As of February 1999, % of the normal level taken as 100%.
[2] Volume of investments (in real terms) in the previous 6 months, as % of the volume of investments in the same period a year ago.
[3] % of total investments.

50%, comparing to 65-70% in other groups. In *ME* and *FE* groups, more firms had investment plans than in the three other groups. Whenever such plans were put in action, they were fulfilled much better in firms controlled by managers or financial outsiders than by any other categories of shareholders.

The composition of investments by source was also remarkably different. Transfer of control over firms to managers or financial outsiders seems to have made access to external financing easier, and its share in total capital outlays in *ME* and *FE* firms was 5-10% higher than in *WE* and *NE* firms. It is important to point out that a similar result was obtained in the 1997 survey (Aukutsionek et al. 1998a; Aukutsionek et al. 1998b). But quite unexpectedly, the highest portion of external financing was then displayed by *SE* firms. Most probably, this was due to subsidies from the state.

While *ME* and *FE* invested almost all their financial resources (85-90%) in machinery and equipment, *WE* and *NE* invested only 65-70%. These data suggest that when control is in the hands of managers or financial outsiders they put a higher priority on modernization and restructuring. However, ways of restructuring chosen by these groups could be different: while *ME* tend to introduce new equipment (almost a half of their capital outlays was invested in the expansion of capacities), *FE* preferred to modernize the existing equipment (their outlays were almost completely invested in major repairs and renewal). It is no less important as a characterization of the attitude of shareholders that, according to managers' own estimates, the expected profitability of investment projects at *ME* and *FE* was one-and-a-half times higher than at *WE* and *NE*. The upper limit of the affordable rate of interest on investment loans was 14-16% in the two former groups, and 9-11% in the latter. However, the lowest profitability was probably typical of investment projects at firms with the state as a dominant shareholder, where the similar indicator was as low as 5%. Quite possibly, the reason was that the major part of their capital outlays was involuntary. Overall, our data provide grounds for the claim that controlling interest by managers or financial outsiders contributed to making investment activity of firms more rational and maintaining it at a higher level. It is important that this finding is in complete agreement with the results of previous REB surveys.[5]

CONCLUDING REMARKS

The system of corporate governance may be regarded as a set of institutional mechanisms that aim to curb deviations from a value-maximizing behavior. While competition in product and factor markets is a disciplining factor, mechanisms of corporate governance constitute in the words of M. Jensen "an early warning system" (Jensen 1993). Since no real economy comes close to the ideal of perfect competition, the selection of inefficient firms through competition in product and factor markets usually takes a long time and involves large-scale waste of resources. The system of corporate governance helps to detect and exterminate wasteful behavior at earlier stages, allowing for substantial saving of resources.

It is well known that in modern Russia, competition in product and factor markets is underdeveloped. In many cases, it is heavily constrained and distorted. Therefore, sorting out inefficient firms here is by far a more troublesome and protracted process than in mature market economies. The situation is still more complicated because many mechanisms of corporate governance are embryonic or even totally absent (Radygin 1996):

- shares of most firms have no quotation in the stock market
- there are many restrictions on free trade in shares

- the market for take-overs is extremely weak
- requirements for disclosure of information are commonly violated
- the existing system of bookkeeping and financial reporting is inconsistent with international standards
- rights of minor shareholders are poorly respected
- court litigation is cumbersome and extremely inefficient
- the volume of bank lending to firms is insignificant, so that monitoring by banks is quite limited
- market for managerial labor is still in its infancy
- boards of directors are mostly controlled by CEO's.

Under such conditions shareholders have no other opportunity to establish effective control over firms except to concentrate large blocks of shares. However, even this may not always be a guarantee of control in the distorted institutional environment of the Russian economy. Nonetheless, this study provides for cautious optimism. REB surveys show a close correlation between the concentration of large blocks of shares in the hands of managers and financial outsiders and better performance by firms. This conclusion, initially drawn from the results of the 1997 survey, was confirmed once more by the 1999 survey. The fact that the composition of surveyed firms in 1997 and 1999 concurred by a third makes our findings even more robust. At the same time, as far as our data show, even this mechanism of control works only in a minor part of Russian firms. It is not surprising that in this situation the behavior of the greater part of firms deviate from the prescriptions of the standards of value-maximization. Unless other components of corporate governance start to work, the present situation in the Russian industry characterized by numerous non-standard forms of behavior by firms may stay unchanged for many years to come.

NOTES

1. If existing ownership structures are the endogenous result of a market process, there would be no visible variations in performance between firms with different types of equity concentration or different groups of largest/dominant shareholders (Demsetz and Lehn 1985; see also: Hansmann 1996). In this case, a market niche will be found for every ownership form wherever its benefits outweigh its costs (Hansmann 1996). However, it is reasonable to expect that in economies under transition the factor of ownership might matter because here ownership structures and patterns of control have not been shaped in the course of a long-term selection process guided by market forces.

2. This classification is different from the classification offered by Earle et al. in one important respect: instead of the conventional division of outside shareholders into institutional and non-institutional groups, they are divided here into financial and non-financial groups. In principle, the point is how to interpret the role and position of one

category of shareholders–"other firms." We believe that in the peculiar Russian environment it is counterproductive and possibly misleading to merge them in a common group with financial institutions. First, in contrast to most financial institutions that appeared under market reforms and belong to the new private sector, the bulk of industrial firms emerged as state-owned firms long before the market reforms began. It is reasonable to suggest that the behavior of agents from the new private sector should largely deviate from the behavior of agents from the former state-owned sector whether they are privatized or still state-owned. Second, cross-shareholding among firms is often used as a barrier against invasion of outsiders. Consequently, it can create opportunities for the "entrenchment" of incumbent managers. This is the reason why we have combined "other firms" with "individual shareholders" in a group of non-financial outsiders that seem to be less capable than financial outsiders to play a role of active (strategic) investors and to initiate deep restructuring.

3. Transfer of a block of shares to subsidiary firms is an effective device to protect a firm from invading outsiders and for this reason it may be treated as an indirect form of managerial ownership. Our data are consistent with this suggestion. Financial outsiders did not hold any significant blocks of shares in firms that were partly owned by their own subsidiaries. The majority of such firms were dominated by insiders and in some cases by the state or non-financial outsiders.

4. Here, redistribution of shares means not just their transfers in the literal sense but also any other changes in the ownership structure such as new flotation, etc.

5. Obviously, our analysis does not give an answer to the crucial question of what is the cause and what is the effect. It may happen that control exercised by managers and financial outsiders is actually a means to improve firm performance. But we cannot rule out that managers and financial outsiders tended to acquire large block of shares of the most successful firms whose performance was better from the outset. For an attempt to solve the problem of causality, see previous REB publications (Aukutsionek et al., 1998a; Aukutsionek et al., 1998b).

REFERENCES

Aukutsionek, S., Kapeliushnikov, R. and Zhukov, V..(1998a). Dominant Shareholders and Performance of Industrial Firms. *The Russian Economic Barometer,* 7(1), 8-41.

Aukutsionek, S., Filatochev, I., Kapelyushnikov, R. and Zhukov, V. (1998b). Dominant Shareholders, Restructuring, and Performance of Privatized Companies in Russia: An Analysis and some Policy Implications. *Communist Economies and Economic Transformation,* 10(6), 495-517.

Berle, A. and Means, G. (1932). *The Modern Corporation and Private Property.* New York: MacMillan.

Demsets, H. and Lehn, K. (1985). The Structure of Corporate Ownership: Causes and Consequences. *Journal of Political Economy,* 93(6), 1155-1177.

Earle, J. S. (1998). Post-Privatization Ownership Structure and Productivity in Russian Industrial Firms. Stockholm, School of Economics, Central European University (draft).

Earle, J. S., Estrin, S. and Leschenko, L. L. (1996). Ownership Structures, Patterns of Control, and Firm Behavior in Russia. In: Commander, S., Fan, Q., and M. Shaffer (eds.) *Firm Restructuring and Economic Policy in Russia.* Washington, DC: The World Bank, EDI.

Earle, J. S. and Estrin, S. (1997). After Voucher Privatization: The Structure and Productivity in Russian Manufacturing Industry. CEPR Discussion Paper.

Hansmann, H. (1996). *The Ownership of Firm.* Cambridge (Mass.): Harvard University Press.

Jensen, M. (1993). The Modern Industrial Revolution, Exit, and the Failure of Internal Control Systems. *Journal of Finance,* 48(3), 4-23.

Kapeliushnikov, R. (1997). Job Turnover in a Transitional Economy: The Behavior and Expectations of Russian Industrial Firms.–In: *Labor Market Dynamics in The Russian Federation,* Paris: OECD.

Morck, R., Shleifer, A. and Vishny, R. (1988). Management Ownership and Market Valuation: An Empirical Analysis. *Journal of Financial Economics,* 20(2), 293-315.

Radygin, A. (1996). *Securities Markets Development and Its Relationship to Corporate Governance in Russia.* Paris: OECD.

Shleifer, A. and Vishny, R. W. (1996). *A Survey of Corporate Governance.* National Bureau of Economic Research, NBER Working Paper No 5554, Cambridge (MA).

Short, H. (1994). Ownership, Control, Financial Structure and Performance of Firms. *Journal of Economic Surveys,* 8(3), 203-249.

SUBMITTED: September 1999
FIRST REVISION: January 2000
SECOND REVISION: May 2000
ACCEPTED: August 2000

The Virtues and Weaknesses
of Insider Shareholding

Olga Kuznetsova
Andrei Kuznetsov

ABSTRACT. Following privatization in Russia, insider shareholders secured supremacy in their companies in most cases. The literature concerned with corporate governance in Russia frequently shows too much affection to the claim that the arrangement when control is allocated to insiders is generally sub-efficient in the long run. It is often concluded that the current pattern of control has negative impact on the progress of reforms. This paper argues in favor of a more balanced view, which takes into account the social responsibility of firms towards stakeholders and the influence the latter have over corporate performance. The question addressed is how real the insiders' threat is in privatized Russian enterprises with regard to the advancement of reforms and development of the workable corporate governance system. *[Article copies available for a fee from The Haworth Document Delivery Service: 1-800-342-9678. E-mail address: <getinfo@haworthpressinc.com> Website: <http://www.HaworthPress.com> © 2001 by The Haworth Press, Inc. All rights reserved.]*

KEYWORDS. Corporate governance, transition economies, Russia, ownership structure, insider shareholding

---

[Haworth co-indexing entry note]: "The Virtues and Weaknesses of Insider Shareholding." Kuznetsova, Olga, and Andrei Kuznetsov. Co-published simultaneously in *Journal of East-West Business* (International Business Press, an imprint of The Haworth Press, Inc.) Vol. 6, No. 4, 2001, pp. 89-106; and: *Russian Corporations: The Strategies of Survival and Development* (ed: Andrei Kuznetsov) International Business Press, an imprint of The Haworth Press, Inc., 2001, pp. 89-106.

SETTING THE PROBLEM

After years of painful reforms the Russian version of the market remains distorted and crippled in comparison to western counterparts. In its present form it looks quite unconventional and yet it is not uncommon that standard concepts reflecting the realities of mature markets are heavily relied upon as a basis for the analysis of the Russian economy.[1] Sometimes this may lead to the misrepresentation of certain trends. This article seeks to demonstrate that the threat of shareholders-insiders to the success of restructuring of Russian corporations may be easily exaggerated if no proper attention is paid to the peculiarities of the Russian business circumstances. The analysis is conducted from the prospective of social cost and social benefit within the constraints of a transitional environment.

The article challenges the opinion that insiders necessarily represent a threat to the speed and advancement of reforms and the introduction of an efficient governance model in Russian firms. It claims that the weakness of institutions prevents insider shareholders from imposing their interests and objectives either as shareholders or as stakeholders. Insider shareholding has not stopped or delayed restructuring if restructuring is defined as the ability of the business organization to adapt to the requirements of the existing business environment. The survival of the thousands of businesses in Russia based on former Soviet state-owned enterprises is the evidence that cannot be disputed. Further alterations in the economic environment will force economic agents to continue to remodel their conduct and organizational arrangements, but not before they feel pressure (either external or internal, or both) for changes.

The transitional economic system is immature from the market prospective. It suffers from loose ties between economic players and the poor quality of economic information, which often lacks sufficient transparency even in the most basic business matters. Institutional deficiency makes it puzzling for market participants to choose priorities and adjust behavior. In turn, the students of transition meet with difficulties evaluating the full range of the aggregate benefits and losses caused by agent's behavioral preferences. The modern Russian corporate system is contradictory but it is not as damaging to the economic performance of corporations as is claimed sometimes (see for example Desai and Golgberg, 2000). Russian companies have proved their ability to cope with the situation of institutional failure applying the strategy of evasion and calculated avoidance of long-term commitments. The social benefit of strategies and behavior responses chosen by the firms outbalance the uninspiring pure economic results calculated in terms of the volume of output or GDP growth.

RUSSIAN CORPORATIONS:
INDISTINCT ENTITIES
WITH AN UNCERTAIN MISSION

Introducing Corporate Governance

It is widely acknowledged that modern corporations have great influence on many aspects of the modern society following the scale of their activities, the political influence they have achieved, their contribution to the national welfare and the internationalization of their operations. In countries like Britain and the USA, for example, the value of listed companies exceeds national GDP. Consequently, a better understanding of the rationale which guides corporations is important to reconcile the interests of corporations and the society and make economic policies more sensible. There is increasing support in the literature to the claim that corporations should contribute to economic growth that makes possible sustainable, equitable and democratic development (Stiglitz, 1998; Nellis, 1999; Fox and Heller, 1999). In other words, there is growing appreciation of the social consequences of economic activities.

One of the forces that allegedly influence corporations is the shareholder. From the point of view of the society shareholders are responsible for imposing on corporate management the requirements of socially meaningful efficiency by demanding a fair return on their assets. This argument was used to justify mass privatization in Russia. However, shareholders may fulfil their social function only in the presence of a certain institutional infrastructure including statutory law and regulations. This infrastructure reflects the concerns of the society regarding corporations and allows shareholders to implement a social function while pursuing their own interests. Such infrastructure was missing in Russia when mass privatization was launched and currently, ten years later, it is still very much not in place. Obviously, this is bound to have very serious consequences as far as the forces affecting corporate governance are concerned. Effectively, privatization and newly evolved ownership patterns have produced a transitional version of the corporate system, which does not require sophisticated market infrastructure and can use expertise developed in the Soviet period.

The weakness of this arrangement is that the Russian society remains deprived of substantive economic advantages that the corporate system developed in the West has to offer. The most prominent areas of concern for business people and academics alike are the lack of transparency in the operations of joint-stock companies, neglect of shareholders rights, the poor compatibility of the government economic policy with the needs of the business community (let alone the population who possess a significant fraction of equity). One of the significant consequences of the inadequate development of the corporate system is growing public mistrust of market institutions (Isaksson, 1999), the factor that can affect the speed of reforms and increase the cost of transformation.

The efficiency of corporate governance, seen here as a mechanism translating signals from product and input markets into corporate behavior (Berglöf and von Thadden, 1999), depends on the degree of development of relevant formal and informal institutions. Corporate governance provides the structure through which the objectives of the company are set and the means of attaining those objectives and monitoring performance are determined. This allows corporations to respond to the expectations of shareholders but not only them. It is now widely recognized that "the competitiveness and ultimate success of a corporation is the result of teamwork that embodies contributions from a range of different resource providers including investors, employees, creditors and suppliers" (OECD Principles of Corporate Governance, 1999). Consequentially, these contributors will be deeply affected by the corporation's success or failure. This puts good corporate governance outside the concern of shareholders alone and into a wider domain that includes the stakeholders of the company as well.

By tuning the mechanism of corporate governance through legislation and other instruments the society can address particular needs of different stakeholders and increase the chance of a socially responsible conduct by corporations as shareholders can find it individually rational to avoid responsibility associated with ownership (Charkham and Simpson, 1999). Russia provides many examples of the indifference of this sort. This may be explained by the absence of incentives for a long-term commitment, as the diffusion of shares among insiders did not create many shareholders with other than marginal influence and involvement.

Conscious shareholding is a phenomenon sequential to the conditions and rules that guide business activities. It is imperative for a responsible equity holding that companies are focused on their objectives, competitive in operations and accountable for their actions. Therefore, we believe that it is extremely important to examine existing incentives and obstacles affecting insider's behavior in modern Russia. Currently very little is known about the cost to the society incurred by the passivity of shareholders-insiders.

Can the Past Be Always Blamed?

The literature quite often blames the legacy of the "pervasive failures" of the command economy for the deficiencies of the modern Russian economy (Brada, 1996). The commonality of this attitude warrants some comment. We do not think that it is constructive as far as corporate governance is concerned for the simple reason that at the micro level there were no or little provisions for this type of relations in the Soviet system. However, there was another type of principle-agent relations at what may be called the macro level that sometimes may be mistaken for proper corporate governance.

During the Soviet period the combined (united) public property was officially proclaimed to be inseparable from the combined (united) proprietor, the public. Consequently, the national economy was conceived and organized as a big household managed from a single center according to a single plan. Hence at the macro level there was room for agency relations, which were never formally acknowledged by the way, as the public property operated through the mechanism of state regulation and control and thus "management" *was* separated from the owner. In terms of corporate governance, the state had acquired the functions of the topmost manager who should protect the interests of the owner, the public.[2] According to theory, however, the manager (the state) requires some special motivations (be it an incentive scheme of any kind or efficient monitoring device) to act in the interest of the owner (the public). Under socialism the "principle" was deprived of the means of control over "executives" as the state and party bureaucracy had succeeded in erecting an insurmountable barrier between themselves and the people. As a result, social and welfare goals and other elements of the public utility function were never sought to be maximized. The major consequence was an economic structure providing little resources for the production of consumer services and goods while concentrating them openly or indirectly in heavy industries and military sectors instead.[3]

These speculations suggest that it is only with serious reservations that "bad inheritance" may be accepted as the source of the malformation of the institute of corporate governance in modern Russia. The "micro-level" corporate governance in Russia is to be created from scratch and this is a historical opportunity that should not be mishandled.

Deceitful Present

In Russia, as everywhere, the economic environment imposes rigorous constraints on the behavior of corporations. What makes the situation unique is the intermediate nature of the economy itself: "most of the Russian economy has not been making progress toward the market or even marking time. It is actively moving in the opposite direction" by choosing to protect itself against the market contrary to the option of accepting it (Gaddy and Ickes, 1998).

In transitional Russia, corporations emerged out of state-owned enterprises. The majority of the latter were immensely big and enjoyed monopolistic advantages. Organizationally and technologically they were tailor-made to fit a very specific economic system. It did not incorporate, like modern capitalist economies, highly developed agency relations. There were no stimuli for the development of certain economic institutions that in western counties alleviate transaction costs in order to overcome externalities of the agency. These institutions, as pointed out by Stiglitz (1999), need to grow incrementally and require decades to evolve. Obviously, Russian firms cannot postpone their operation till after this process is complete. It is no wonder then that in circumstances of institutional uncertainty, which are more propitious for stealing then producing, less complicated relations and organizational forms prove to be more attractive. In practice this means that in the situation of institutional collapse a governance system that requires less advanced institutional support can be more efficient as a tool of running a firm then more sophisticated arrangements. An organization prevailed by insiders who have obtained ownership rights without incurring any cost or putting in a noticeable effort may well be such an initial form of corporation. Organizationally, it has not moved far away from its predecessor, the state-owned enterprise, and therefore could be managed with existing expertise.

DISAMBIGUATING TRANSITIONAL CHALLENGES

To set up the point of reference for our further analysis we have to evaluate the developments in the area of corporate governance from the point of view of their contribution to the success of market reforms. It is necessary to decide first what should be counted as a positive result and what as negative. We need to identify then whether what has been achieved is in any relation to a particular model of corporate governance or whether the role of corporate governance was no more then figurative.

However, the success or failure of reforms cannot be evaluated in economic terms alone. Post communist transition is as much about emerging societies as it is about emerging economies. We agree with Birman (1996) and Stiglitz (1999) who emphasize that the creation of a market economy should be viewed as a mean to secure broader objectives. As Stiglitz (1999, p.12) wrote: "It is not just the creation of a market economy that matters, but the improvement of living standards and the establishment of the foundations of sustainable, equitable, and democratic development." Therefore the development of social norms and institutions, social capital and trust are critically important as well. The design of economic objectives should reflect socially acceptable values. At the same time the definition of a socially responsible behavior for corporations will have different meaning and scope in a mature market economy and a transitional economy. A distinct feature of the latter is that the institutional disorder contributes heavily to the complexity of the business environment as the "rules of engagement" are not clearly set. Under these circumstances, it is more difficult to formulate and make noticeable social demands for business as well as allocate responsibility for their fulfillment.

Successful corporate performance is the justification of and the remuneration for efficient corporate governance. With regard to economies in transition a number of important questions have never been answered (and possibly have never been asked): What is the social criterion (i.e., shared by the society during a particular historical period) of the efficient corporation in terms of achievements, responsibility and conduct? If the mass privatization in Russia was launched with the purpose to create preconditions for democracy, has it led to establishing corporations capable of assuming socially justifiable economic policies? How can corporate governance help corporations in achieving socially significant goals?

Russian mass privatization was first and foremost politically motivated. There was talk about "liberating" the market forces and creating "effective owners" in the interests of the best employment of assets (Chubais and Vishnevskaya, 1993), but these developments were compromised as the reformers showed little concern for putting together the infrastructure and institutions of the market. As it happened, the "liberation" made rich a very small group of people, while enterprises and their employees were left to struggle for survival. The class of "effective owners" has failed to become prominent. As Charkham and Simpson (1999) put it, the possession of an umbrella is not the same as the ownership of British Telecom shares. The latter requires matching institutions and mechanisms. In their absence, it is little surprise that newly-created corporations in Russia have offered so far no definitive proof of the superiority of the market mechanism of resources allocation over central planning: the absolute majority of privatized firms are poor performers or loss makers. Most "prosperous" companies belong to natural monopolies and can hardly be evidence of the success of the new order.

In Russia, the performance of privatized firms defies theoretical forecasts, prognosticating that the output dynamics in transitional countries would follow a U-shaped curve (Blanchard, 1997). Most firms retain excessive labor and invest inefficiently (Kapelyushnikov, 1998; Batyaeva and Aukutsionek, 1999). Many are closed joint stock companies, just few hundred are listed on the stock exchange and only dozens see any trading in their shares. In this context the expression "to go public" has acquired certain irony when applied to Russian corporations. They are not particularly keen on any disclosure and idiosyncratic to the "more transparency" claim, which instead of recalling association with external investors, make them think about bankruptcy.

The delay in institution building has obviously created additional difficulties for the advancement of reforms. Firms reacted by opting for a survival strategy based on the calculated avoidance of long-term commitments and structural adjustments for the sake of a short-term gain. The society depends on corporations but lack of the mechanisms of corporate control interferes with establishing understanding and trust between the two. More scrupulous economic policy and new institutions are required to merge business interests and the societal interest in sustainable development.

SHARE OF SHARES OR SHARE OF CONTROL?

Changes in the Structure of Shareholding

Let us turn to the issue of Russian corporation's progress in terms of ownership structure and performance. The privatization procedures advantaged insiders. As a result, employees usually hold the largest cut of shares (Table 1).

Since the end of the mass privatization the distribution of shares between insiders has been shifting in favor of managers. The proportion of external shareholders remains low despite some noticeable growth.[4] Institutional involvement has not taken off yet. Banks generally show little interest in shareholding although a few of them have become centers of substantial financial-industrial groups. The state remains a prominent shareholder in a considerable number of firms.

Firm managers are a particularly prominent group of shareholders. According to some sources, initially they acquired about 7% of all equity distributed during privatization in Russia. In consequent years this share increased to up to 10-12% and in some cases incumbent managers reserved for themselves up to 50% of the company's shares (Jones, 1998; Blasi and Shleifer, 1996). Our own analysis of the data collected by REB reveals a similar trend: management staff as a group own on average 33% of shares.

The implications of the prevalence of insiders are manifold. First, it set up a backdrop for the development of the system of corporate governance in the country. Second, it highlighted the conflict of interests between shareholders-insiders and shareholders-outsiders. Third, this created an environment favorable for integrating the interests of different groups of insiders at least during the early phase of the evolution of corporate governance in Russia. Forth, privatization legitimized the influence and control acquired by "Red Directors" during the pre-reforms era.

Theorists are generally quite critical about the structure of corporate ownership in Russia. It is believed to have led to managerial entrenchment, rent seek-

TABLE 1. Structure of Equity Holding in Russian Joint-Stock Companies After Privatization and in 1999 (%)

	After privatization	1999
1. Internal (total)	66	51.3
Employees	47	36.6
Administration	19	15
Collective trust	–	–
2. External (total)	10	45.3
Banks	–	1.7
Suppliers, buyers, other firms holdings, FIGs*	–	3.4
Individuals	3	15.6
Foreign investors	–	7.6
Investment funds	3	5.2
Others	–	0.7
3. State	20	2.7
Total	100	100

* FIGs - Financial-Industrial Groups
Source: A. Radygin "Ownership and Control of the Russian Industry" OECD/USAID Conference on Corporate Governance in Russia. Moscow, 31 May-2 June 1999.

ing and labor hoarding, which discourage external investors and diminish long-term prospects for company restructuring and market adaptation (Blasi et al., 1997, Frydman et al., 1996; Filatochev, 1997).

Although this criticism is generally well grounded, it falls short of grasping the whole range of specific factors characteristic of the transition process in Russia and therefore is not entirely correct. The failure of the manufacturing sector to restructure calls for a more complex explanation than just references to the selfishness and incompetence of firm managers or pressure by workers. There are reasons to believe that the impact of insider shareholding on the reforms is more neutral then damaging. As the first step towards proving this it is essential to establish if the accumulation of ownership rights by insiders has been matched with the adequate distribution of controlling power. Research demonstrates in fact that in Russia (a) control is more concentrated than ownership; (b) control and ownership may be well separated. As a source of control, ownership matters in Russia only to the extent it is underpinned with power associated with the position of authority in as much as extra-ownership control is highly effective. Employees as a group may own over 60 per cent of all shares, but as individuals, the overwhelming majority have only an insignificant number of shares.

What is clear is that small shareholders have little power to influence corporate policy and that they are restricted in their ability to exercise their own rights in full. It would be naïve, then, to expect shareholders not to be aware of this and adjust their behavior accordingly. There are only few examples of shareholders-employees to take consorted action. Mostly this category of shareholders is quite inert, possibly because the cost of monitoring managers is too high for dispersed shareholders in the atmosphere of secrecy prevailing in Russia.

Dispersed shareholding requires more rigorous institutional support to be consequential. In Russia, however, the mechanism of the legal protection of shareholder rights is still in infancy and the culture of equity holding is lacking. In any corporate system, the ability of small shareholders to exercise control is negligible unless they find ways to agree on common goals and act jointly to achieve them (Carberry, 1996). In Russia, small shareholders have even fewer resources and incentives to execute their right of control over corporate assets and policy (Kuznetsov and Kuznetsova, 1996). Therefore, it is not the insiders' shareholding that represents a real threat to the success of reforms, but the deficiency of institutions providing support to scattered shareholding.

Employee Ownership?

In joint-stock companies, the distribution of ownership rights is not equal to the distribution of control. Hence, a simple reference to the total share of the equity allocated to insiders does not get one really far in understanding the balance of forces as far as the controlling power of various groups of shareholders is concerned. Besides, there is evidence in the literature (Carberry, 1996) that an extensive employee ownership does not usually translate into employee involvement in corporate-level decisions; their voting rights are rarely used as a means to gain influence; even when employees do have a significant role in governance, this does not lead to drastic changes in corporate policy. We tried to find evidence in REB surveys that workers abused their shareholder rights and influenced the firm policy so as to protect their interests as stakeholders (i.e., the firm's employees). As REB data show, enterprises with labor overhang mention pressure from workers-shareholders as an obstacle for redundancies in no more then five per cent of cases (Kapelyushnikov, 1998). In the first half of 1999, with the assistance of REB, we approached 116 firms with the question, "Who does define the priorities in areas related to the performance of the firm?" The respondents (enterprise managers) were asked to put 100 if the director of the enterprise is solely responsible for the decisions and 0 if he is not involved in the process of decision-making at all. The results show that directors enjoy almost unchecked discretion in decision-making:

Decisions concerning	Now	In 3-4 years time
Price	66	59
Production	73	69
Financial	80	73
Employment	75	68
Wage	82	77
Investment	82	75
R&D	80	71
Privatization, restructuring, structural adjustment	70	64

These figures suggest that despite the prevalence of insiders, there is no employee-ownership in Russia in a "traditional" sense. The combined number of shares held by workers in respect to the number held by other shareholders may be substantial, but individual possessions are likely to be very small and there is little evidence that insider shareholders co-ordinate their actions. This perception conforms with the claim of Lissovolik (1997) that, in reality, shareholding in Russia is scattered among investors in contrast to the widely-held perception that concentrated blocks of stakes rule the companies here. Similarly there are no data available yet that allow maintaining that the decision-making power concentrated in the hands of managers is the reflection of their position as shareholders. In fact, "employee-ownership system" requires as much institutional support as any other system of corporate governance. Mass privatization did not provide for these institutions as it did not provide for institutional foundations of outsider control.

PAIN AND GAIN OF THE INSIDER SHAREHOLDER

The interests of insider shareholders are influenced by circumstances that may be both external and internal to their firms. In Russia, the business environment for industrial firms has been very challenging and even hostile. The government failed to help the national industry to adjust to the requirements of the unplanned economy and countervail the onslaught of international competition. At the same time, up to August 1998, short-term financial speculations had been made so lucrative that no investor was willing to consider other options. As a result, strategic shareholders-outsiders have been a rarity.

Faced with the threats of a transitional market, insider shareholders had no difficulty identifying what was their distinctive long-term group interest. As the labor market shrank and the mobility of labor remained very low, employees had a vested interest in keeping their enterprise operational, as they regarded it as the provider of the means for their livelihood. Noticeably, these means never came as dividends or return on the sale of shares, because as a rule, shares are not liquid and dividends have never been either paid or, if paid, significant. Wages, although often delayed, and benefits in kind provided by enterprises determined that the interests of insiders as employees overwhelmed their interests as shareholders. This situation was likely to urge them to support decisions that would make them better off as stakeholders while probably making them worse off as shareholders.

Privatization did not change organizational routines much, except that the perspectives of managerial employment became conditional to a slightly different set of regulations and arrangements. Experience and authority gained by incumbents under central planning has not lost its relevance completely, inasmuch as old skills are better than none, but more importantly, because sluggish reforms failed to make these skills obsolete. According to our data, the average number of years current directors were in charge in the surveyed enterprises was nine and their average age was 50. Understandably, in the absence of a proper job market for this category of specialists, the opportunity for horizontal or vertical job mobility is extremely restricted. Our survey indicates only very limited turnover among management staff, the only significant reasons for dismissal revealed being retirement age and voluntary withdrawal. Under these circumstances, the protection of their own status has become a strong motivation of managerial behavior and, often, opportunism. This implies the choice between two possible types of conduct. One, the "survival" type of response, will aim at keeping the company afloat at any cost, gaining support of the work collective and important stakeholders. The other will seek to exploit short-term opportunities supplied by the infant market and prioritize assets stripping and rent-seeking, usually with deadly consequences for the firm concerned.

Interestingly, managers who started their jobs in the 1990's demonstrate similarity to the pre-reform generation of directors in values, behavioral norms and even priorities. Moreover, the share of managers with revealed pro-market orientation, although small overall, is higher in those enterprises in which old management was retained (Aukutsionek, 1997). This is a strong piece of evidence in favor of the claim that social and economic constraints determine managerial attitudes in the first place. At the same time, there is little manifestation that either managers or workers who gained a major share of equity capital during privatization have acquired awareness characteristic of shareholders in the West (Blasi et al., 1997). Managers and workers of privatized firms appear to share interests more as stakeholders rather than shareholders as for the majority of employees equity ownership is little more than a formality which, at least at present, has hardly any impact on their life. In Russia, the rights to vote do not necessarily secure economic benefits associated with shareholding, as a shareholder retains proportional voting rights, which do not necessarily correspond to the company's value. Even large investors owning a blocking minority stake in a company find it difficult to enforce proportional economic interest (Corporate Governance in Russia, 1999).

In fact, post-communist privatization caught the employees and managers of state-owned enterprises as unprepared as the rest of the population. In the West, the decision to buy out is taken by interested parties voluntarily, either to facilitate the restructuring of troubled firms, or to release efficiencies which require the full commitment of insiders (Thompson and Wright, 1995). By contrast, in transition economies, to name just a few differences, "buy outs" were imposed by governments on sound and ailing firms alike, on political grounds, mainly. For the insiders, becoming owners of their enterprises was not so much the issue of increasing efficiency and returns as preserving their very livelihood in a hostile and uncertain environment. In a short run, financial incentives appear to be of less interest for Russian managers than the considerations of securing their own position in the hierarchy of the newly privatized firm.

FROM CONTINGENCY TOWARDS PROBABILITY

It is common that the efficiency of firms controlled by insiders is put in question in the literature on the grounds that they lack mechanisms to check the possible abuse of power by managers. This argument loses some of its poignancy in countries like Russia, in which such mechanisms are equally absent in firms under outsider control as well, following the general paralysis of the law enforcement system. The impact of legal regulation depends not so much on what is regulated but on what can be enforced: if the enforcement instruments are missing, legal protection is of little help to those entitled. The potency of the legal system is just one example of forces external to the firm that are instrumental in shaping the pattern of control allocation within the firm. If these forces fail to make their impact noticeable, the internal structures of the firm must assume functions that would allow it to adapt to such failure. They may also be forces to assume some faculties, which are plethoric for them and would be placed elsewhere in other situations. This enhances the role of insiders while making them less receptive to signals from outside their organization. With this, the scope of the social responsibility of corporations gets narrower and reflects the interests of those internal to the corporations or strongly associated with them. In other words, the situation favors stakeholders.

That stakeholders appear to have a stronger grip over firms than shareholders is often regarded as a serious weakness of the system of corporate governance in Russia. The domination of top managers in particular is seen as a major setback for reforms. But as soon as one accepts that a survival strategy has been a prime option for Russian firms as determined by the economic environment, the evaluation of managerial performance shifts its emphasis. The drive of top managers towards concentrating economic power emerges as a rational choice motivated by the weakness or absence of some important market institutions and operational systems, in particular, that shareholders as formal owners are not able to take a lead as a strategic force. By contrast, the interest of stakeholders is more emphatic. Under these circumstances, what may appear as "the abuse of power" in terms of standard organizational theory comes out as a rational response to existing constraints. These constraints include, apart from the weakness of market institutions mentioned earlier, the conservation of many features of the pre-reform economic mechanism. The paradox of the Russian corporate system is that, due to inconsistent reforms, the mechanisms of the market are still too inadequate to subdue firms to their discipline thus leaving them to rely on now obsolete practices, as well as the intuition and the experience of managers. Actually, dependence on networks and kin ties, avoidance to rise capital from outside the company is not a Russian-specific feature but a common type of behavior brought about by the inoperative for commercial purposes environment (Miwa and Ramseyer, 1999). It is not impossible that concentration of shares in the hands of insiders and managers in particular will have a positive impact in a long run. Shareholding encourages the development of a long-term commitment to the firm and may interfere with the impulses pushing towards funneling resources and assets stripping. What will tip the balance is the success in putting together institutions that will provide the shareholders with the mechanisms of monitoring and intervention, thus facilitating owner's control, whatever the ownership structure.

CONCLUSIONS

A more balanced approach to the impact on transition of insider shareholding is necessary if the full account is taken of the fact that Russia lacks a basic market infrastructure and regulatory framework. Market institutions and market relations, such as the contract, for example, often bear only superficial resemblance to their counterparts in mature market conditions.

Privatization made self-defense the motor of managerial behavior. To support the continuation of their tenure managers had no choice but to seize the leadership by concentrating efforts on enterprise survival, reaching the internal consensus and consolidating power through personal shareholding. In advanced capitalist countries the allocation of shares to managers is used normally to set additional incentives for managerial performance. By contrast for Russian managers owning stocks is neither incentive, nor compensation.

Furthermore, they have to respond to a very specific economic environment characterized inter alia with the following features:

- the collapse of the national economy has turned Russia to a great extent into a "moneyless society" as over 50 per cent of all transactions between firms take place in a form of barter;
- employees are either not paid wages for months or urged to take the products of their firms as payment;
- the stock market is not an instrument that helps capital to flow to the most attractive sectors of the economy from the least attractive. A World Bank publication (Lieberman, and Kirkness, 1998) points at poor implementation of even basic rules on trading, little or no protection for shareholder rights. With little or no activity in most shares, stock quotations and prices often do not reflect the prices at which transactions would take place;
- a new type of ownership was created through the process of voucher distribution. Individuals obtained ownership rights without injecting any capital of their own, hence, the majority are not investors in the proper sense of the word;
- the culture of committed shareholding is missing.

Clearly, these conditions could not but affect the nature of responsibilities of corporate executives to their shareholders and the allocation of priorities by firms with regard to the corporate performance. The distinction between the shareholder and the stakeholder is blurred, as the major group of shareholders is identical to the major group of stakeholders. At the same time, standard financial indicators like revenue, debt, dividends, the price of shares, due to market inefficiency, become too arbitrary to carry any constructive information. As a result, the role of external shareholders is insignificant as they find it equally difficult either to make up their mind about company performance or to make their will known to corporate executives. Meanwhile, with the feeble stock market capable of generating only weak signals, executives are more likely to bow to pressures from inside the firm (Kuznetsov and Kuznetsova, 1996).

The following circumstances make managers particularly receptive to internal influences:

- the paternalistic role traditionally played by Russian managers towards their workforce (Clarke, 1995);
- dependence on important local informal networks (Kuznetsova and Kuznetsov, 1996);
- susceptibility to coercion on the part of regional government as a result of the political weakness of the center and inadequate legal protection;
- the questionable legality of ownership rights (Glazyev, 2000);
- the realization that the government would be more prepared to bail out ailing firms if the latter play an important role as providers of social services to local communities.

With the informational function of the stock market in disarray, control by stakeholders is the only way to keep corporations socially responsive and managers accountable. Increasing shareholder's wealth may be a legitimate criterion of efficiency in performing market systems. In the midst of a deep economic crisis, Russian firms are preoccupied with survival. Revealed stakeholder's interests provide managers with a set of socially significant reference marks within which they are able to maximize the short-term performance of their firms but also pursue some social goals, which might not be intrinsically a part of a business enterprise. Paternalism of the Russian managers inherited from the Soviet system has brought about positive results by having smoothed social tension and offering shelter to socially exposed citizens. It also substitutes for otherwise absent informal (like in the USA) or formal (like in Germany) internal structures that allow employees to influence corporate decision-making from the shop floor. REB surveys helped to establish paternalistic attitudes as one of the main factors of labor hoarding at Russian enterprises (Kapelyushnikov, 1998). The last factor seems to be particularly important having been mentioned by 51 per cent of respondents.

While the literature on Russian transition routinely criticizes managers for calculated avoidance of long-term adjustments, the approach taken by this paper suggests that environmental constraints should take their part of blame too. As for Russia, existing constraints require that a whole set of definitions must be revised if and when they are applied to this country. The very criterion of the efficient corporation needs some updating. For example, the one inherent in the Anglo-Saxon paradigm, on the growth of the wealth of shareholders, loses its lure in the Russian context. Managers cannot be expected to fulfil the impossible mission of pursuing meaningless goals. Further more, the strain of a transitional process places a bias on the issue of social responsibility of corporations, their ability to contribute to the shaping of a new society rather than simply behave "properly" in a new type of economy. Insider shareholding cannot stop or delay restructuring more than the business environment can stop or delay it.

NOTES

1. Thus, Gaddy and Ickes (1998), who found an innovative analytical approach, were more successful in explaining some unconventional outcomes of the Russian transition than many of their colleagues.

2. Such an approach provides another interesting angle for analysis: post-communist transition as a transformation of a Russian economy as a bankrupt corporation. See: J. Stiglitz and D. Ellerman "New Bridges Across the Chasm: Macro- and Micro-Strategies for Russia." Paper presented at the ECR panel on the Russian economy, January 8, 2000, Boston, USA.

3. Igor Birman and Alec Nove contributed immensely to this disclosure.

4. There are speculations supported mainly with anecdotal evidence, though, that the increase of the outsider holdings was the result of cross-holdings with significant managerial involvement.

REFERENCES

Aukutsionek, S. (1997). Measuring Progress towards a Market Economy. *Communist Economies & Economic Transformation,* 9 (2), 161-162.

Batyaeva, A. and Aukutsionek S. (1999). Investment and Non-Investment in the Russian Industry. *The Russian Economic Barometer,* VIII (4), 3-23.

Berglöf, E. and von Thadden E.-L. (1999). "The Changing Corporate Governance Paradigm: Implications for Transition and developing Countries." Paper presented at the Annual Bank Conference on Developmemt Economies-Europe (ABCDE) "Governance, Equity and Global Markets," June 21-23, 1999, Paris.

Birman, I. (1996). Gloomy Prospects for the Russian Economy. *Europe-Asia Studies,* 48 (5), 735-750.

Blanchard, O. (1997). *The Economics of Post-Communist Transition.* Oxford: Clarendon Press.

Blasi, J.R., Kroumova, M., and Kruse, D. (1997). *Kremlin Capitalism.* London: Cornell University Press.

Brada, J.C. (1996). Corporate Governance in Transition Economies: Lesson from Recent Developments in OECD Member Countries. OECD, Paris.

Carberry, E. J. (1996). Corporate Governance In Employee-Ownership Companies. *The Corporate Board,* September/October, 15-20.

Charkham, J. and Simpson, A. (1999). *Fair Shares. The Future of Shareholder Power and Responsibility.* New York: Oxford University Press Inc., 275 pp.

Chubais, A., and Vishnevskaya M. (1993). Main Issues of Privatization in Russia. Reprinted in Åslund A. (ed.) *Russia's Economic Transformation in the 1990's.* London and Washington: Pinter, 1997. ·

Clarke, S. (ed.) (1995) *Management and Industry in Russia.* London: Edward Elgar.

Corporate Governance in Russia: Cleaning up the Mess (1999). Troika Dialog Research, May. Moscow, 119 pp.

Desai, R.M. and Golgberg, I. (2000). The Vicious Circles of Control. Regional Governments and Insiders in Privatized Russian Enterprises. *Policy Research Working Paper* (2247). The World Bank. Europe and Central Asia Region. Private and Financial Sectors Development Union. Washington, DC, USA, 23 pp.

Filatochev, I. (1997). "Privatization and Corporate Governance" Review Article. *World Economy,* 20(4), 497-510.

Fox, M.B. and Heller, M.A.(1999). Lessons From Fiascos in Russian Corporate Governance (Paper #99-012). University of Michigan Law School, William Davidson Institute.

Frydman, R., Gray, C. and Rapaczynski, A. (eds.) (1996). *Corporate Governance in Central Europe and Russia.* Vol. 1 and 2–Budapest: CEU Press.

Gaddy, C. and Ickes, B. (1998). Russia's Virtual Economy. *Foreign Affairs.* 77(5), 53-67.

Glazyev, S. (2000). Interview with Sergei Glazyev, Chairman of the Duma Committee on Economic Policies and Entrepreneurship. *Vek,* No. 5 (370), February.

Isaksson, M. (1999). *Investment, Financing and Corporate Governance: The Role and Structure of Corporate Governance Arrangements in OECD Countries.* OECD, USAID and World Bank Conference. Moscow, 31 May-2 June 1999.

Kapelyushnikov, R. (1998). "Chto skryvaets'a za "skritoy bezrabotitsey"?" in T. Maleeva (Ed.): *State and Corporate Employment Policy.* Moscow, Carnegie Endowment for International Peace, pp. 75-111.

Kuznetsov, A. and Kuznetsova, O. (1996). Privatization, Shareholding and the Efficiency Argument: Russian Experience. *Europe-Asia Studies,* 48(7), 1173-85.

Kuznetsova, O. and Kuznetsov, A. (1996). From a Socialist Enterprise to a Capitalist Firm: The Hazards of the Managerial Learning Curve. *Communist Economies & Economic Transformation,* 8(4), 517-528.

Kuznetsova, O. and Kuznetsov, A. (1999). The State as a Shareholder: Responsibilities and Objectives. *Europe-Asia Studies,* 51(3), 433-446.

Lieberman, I.W. and Kirkness C.D. (1998). *Privatization and Emerging Equity Markets.* Washington: World Bank.

Miwa, Y. and Ramseyer, J.M. (1999). The Value of Prominent Directors: Lessons in Corporate Governance from Transitional Japan. Paper presented at the William Davidson Institute, The University of Michigan Law School, September 1999.

Nellis, J. (1999). Time to Rethink Privatization in Transition Economies? *Transition,* 10(1), 4-6.

OECD General Principles of Company Law for Transition Economies (1999). *The Journal of Corporation Law,* 24(2) (Winter), 190-293.

OECD Principles of Corporate Governance (1999). OECD, Directorate for Financial, Fiscal and Enterprise Affairs. Paris. http://www.oecd.org/daf/governance/principles.htm

Thompson, S. and Wright, M. (1995). Corporate Governance–The Role of Restructuring Transactions. *Economic Journal,* 105(430), 690-703.

Stiglitz, J. (1998) More Instruments and Broader Goals: Moving towards the Post-Washington Consensus. WIDER Annual Lecture, The United Nations University, Helsinki.

Stiglitz, J. (1999). Wither Reforms? Ten Years of the Transition. Keynote address at the Annual Conference of the World Bank on Development Economics, April 28-30, Washington.

SUBMITTED: January 2000
FIRST REVISION: June 2000
SECOND REVISION: August 2000
ACCEPTED: August 2000

Index

Printed in the United States
by Baker & Taylor Publisher Services